CREDIT RATING AGENC

Finance Matters

Series Editors: Kathryn Lavelle, Case Western Reserve University, Cleveland, Ohio and Timothy J. Sinclair, University of Warwick

This series of books provides advanced introductions to the processes, relationships and institutions that make up the global financial system. Suitable for upper-level undergraduate and taught graduate courses in financial economics and the political economy of finance and banking, the series explores all aspects of the workings of the financial markets within the context of the broader global economy.

Published

Banking on the State: The Political Economy of Public Savings Banks
Mark K. Cassell

British Business Banking: The Failure of Finance Provision for SMEs
Michael Lloyd

Credit Rating Agencies
Giulia Mennillo

The European Central Bank
Michael Heine and Hansjörg Herr

Quantitative Easing: The Great Central Bank Experiment
Jonathan Ashworth

Regulating Banks: The Politics of Instability
Andrew Whitworth

CREDIT RATING AGENCIES

GIULIA MENNILLO

agenda
publishing

I dedicate this book to my son, Vincent Elias, who taught me where the true source of inspiration, curiosity and perseverance lies.

© Giulia Mennillo 2022

First published in 2022 by Agenda Publishing

Agenda Publishing Limited
The Core
Bath Lane
Newcastle Helix
Newcastle upon Tyne
NE4 5TF
www.agendapub.com

ISBN 978-1-78821-192-5 (hardcover)
ISBN 978-1-78821-193-2 (paperback)

British Library Cataloguing-in-Publication Data
A catalogue record for this book is available from the British Library

Typeset by Newgen Publishing UK
Printed and bound in the UK by CPI Group (UK) Ltd, Croydon, CR0 4YY

CONTENTS

ACKNOWLEDGEMENTS

This book would not have been written without the support of many accompanying me along the way. I want to thank the colleagues at the Department of Political Science at the National University of Singapore (NUS) for providing an academic home in which I could write and teach. I want to thank my brilliant students who attended my global political economy classes and my honours seminar on the politics of global finance. Their interest and curiosity challenged and encouraged me to write this book. I feel humbled and thankful that I could share my fascination about the social and political character of financial markets with them. My thanks also for their research assistance go to my former student Martin Indrawata at NUS and to Sophie Behrendt who interned at the Akademie für Politische Bildung in Tutzing (Germany), my new employer on the old continent.

I owe a debt of gratitude to Soo Yeon Kim, for being an ever-attentive mentor during my time at NUS. Further, I am incredibly grateful to the editors of the *Finance Matters* series, Kathryn Lavelle and Timothy J. Sinclair. They gave me a unique opportunity to publish part of my work on credit rating agencies in a book. I also want to thank Alison Howson from Agenda Publishing for her patience and her editing efforts of my (sometimes German) English and to Mike Richardson for the sharp-eyed copy-editing.

Thank you also to Mary Rose Blanco, for providing so much support and help at home. Many thanks also to Sabina Glaser, for the many inspiring conversations. Thanks to Chatsworth Preschool, for providing a stimulating learning and playing environment for my son. I owe immense thanks to Mara Victoria, who is a true bundle of joy and a great co-worker. Last not but not least, deepest thanks to Björn, my husband, for being my backbone with his love, while bearing my weaknesses and vulnerabilities.

Giulia Mennillo

FIGURES AND TABLES

FIGURES

TABLES

LIST OF ABBREVIATIONS

BCA	Baseline Credit Assessment
BCBS	Basel Committee on Banking Supervision
CEBS	Committee of European Banking Supervisors
CESR	Committee of European Securities Regulators
CQS	Credit Quality Step
CRA	Credit Rating Agency
CRD	Capital Requirements Directive
CSRC	China Securities Regulatory Commission
ECAF	Eurosystem credit assessment framework
ECAI	External Credit Assessment Institutions
ESG	Environmental, Social, and Governance
ESMA	European Securities and Markets Authority
ESME	European Securities Markets Expert Group
ETF	Exchange Traded Fund
FC	Foreign Currency
FSB	Financial Stability Board
IDR	Issuer Default Rating
IOSCO	International Organization of Securities Commissions
LC	Local Currency
LT	Long Term
NDRC	National Development and Reform Commission
NRSRO	Nationally Recognized Statistical Rating Organization
OCR	Office of Credit Ratings

PBOC	People's Bank of China
RLG	Regional and Local Governments
SEC	US Securities and Exchange Commission
SOE	State-owned Enterprise
S&P	S&P Global Ratings
TTC	Through the Cycle

INTRODUCTION

Credit rating agencies (CRAs) are of consequence far beyond the world of finance. Before the global financial crisis (GFC) few outside academia and the financial industry had heard of them, but their role in the credit crunch of 2008 catapulted them onto the front pages of newspapers, where their practices became an issue for scrutiny. As time has passed, and the catastrophe of the systemic global financial crisis of 2008 has receded into history, lessons about the far-reaching relevance of key financial market actors, such as credit rating agencies, have faded. Once investment bankers, accountancy companies, private equity firms, hedge funds and other creatures associated with Wall Street and "casino capitalism" (Strange 1986) disappear from the pages of the major media outlets, policy-makers, the general public and large sections of academia relegate issues pertinent to finance to a technicality, leaving deeper analytical engagement to specialists, quants or experts. The ambition of this book is to bring credit rating agencies and their role in the economy back into focus, offering a more holistic understanding of the agencies and their ratings. In addition to introducing basic and important terms and concepts, this book pays tribute to the often neglected political and social dimension of the agencies' work and the authority that comes with it.

Credit rating agencies are private firms, whose core business is to assess the creditworthiness of debt issuers on financial markets. The famous alphanumeric codes, such as AAA, BB+ and Baa3, can decide the fate of a company or a whole country. The long-standing credit rating agency oligopoly of the Big Three – namely Standard & Poor's Global Ratings, Moody's Investors Service and Fitch Ratings – dominates the global rating market.

Financial products that carry ratings, in most cases, involve some type of debt issuance by funding-seeking entities. "Bonds" represent the most common form of such products.[1] The related debt can be issued by a number of entities: private companies (corporates), financial institutions (banks), governments (sovereigns), supranationals (e.g. the World Bank Group) and subnational institutions (e.g. municipalities). When these entities seek access to capital markets in order to satisfy their funding needs, the assigned rating signals to investors the extent to which the debt issuer is "creditworthy" – literally, "worthy" of receiving capital. In addition, credit rating agencies also rate structured financial products such as securitized mortgages, generally referred to as "asset-backed securities".

Despite the criticism CRAs faced in the context of the 2008 global financial crisis in terms of conflicts of interest, rating failure and timeliness, there is a persistent reliance on CRA ratings by market participants. Investors, debt issuers and public and regulatory authorities such as central banks and financial supervisors continue to use credit ratings for delegating credit risk assessment.[2] Credit rating agencies are anything but discredited players in today's financial markets, and remain as important as ever. Their ratings are pivotal for the system to work. The agencies' crisis resilience and the indispensability of their ratings to financial market practices demonstrate that these institutions are constitutive players in global financialized capitalism.[3] Most conventional readings of the CRAs' role underplay this aspect and thus miss one half of the story. The purpose of this book is to convey the full story. Focusing on a purely functional understanding, in which ratings exist only to reduce information asymmetries in the market, has its shortcomings. It neglects the embeddedness of CRAs "in networks of social interest representation" (Sinclair 1999: 158): "[Although CRAs] do not represent the interests of globalizing elites in a conscious, conspiratorial fashion, battling the evil hordes of the welfare state and socialism, ... rating is an ideology in that its assumptions privilege a system of values and knowledge tied to particular social forces." Reducing the role of rating to the lessening of information asymmetries underplays the political and power dynamics at play. Interactions between the rating, the rated entity and the rating audience, which includes not only investors and analysts but also journalists, policy-makers, regulators and the general public, go by the board. Ratings shape investors' perceptions of the creditworthiness of bond issuers, and thus influence investment decisions and direct capital flows. Furthermore, there is a normative impact of ratings on rated entities – whether states or corporations – which are induced to adjust according to the rating criteria in order to rank more highly and enjoy favourable access to credit. The scholarly literature refers to this imperative of anticipatory obedience as the credit rating agencies' "structural power" (see Chapter 1).

Ratings are not merely reflections or "cameras" taking snapshots of the creditworthiness of a product, firm or country. They act like an "engine"; they are performative (MacKenzie 2006). In the case of nation states, ratings can determine the fiscal room for manoeuvre, shape the economic policy agenda and facilitate or limit the role of the state in the economy. Not least, they can have governance effects with distributional consequences, as CRAs promote policy norms that follow a similar inner logic within the corporate and governmental world.

Consider the examples of toll bridges and the privatization of railroads. The toll and higher train ticket prices may pay for themselves. Economically speaking, it may look less risky to finance these services through consumer pricing instead of through general taxation. For this reason, such arrangements of public good infrastructure contribute to a more favourable credit rating from the CRAs. At first sight, such an assessment may appear objective and apolitical. But, on closer examination, tolls and expensive train tickets hurt the lower income strata proportionally more in a society. Just like VAT, they are an indirect and regressive form of taxation. Even though the norms CRAs promote may appear as a legitimate and impartial representation of investors' interests, rating creates winners and losers in society. Its governance effects are undeniably politically salient.

For example, the sovereign rating downgrades of developed countries in the wake of the GFC between 2007 and 2010 induced a focused problematization of sovereign creditworthiness. The main rating drivers of the downgrades were public finances, especially deficits, gross public debt and the general macroeconomic situation and growth (International Monetary Fund [IMF] 2010: 103).[4] This made us forget the very cause of the massive increases of public debt: the bail-out of banks and the necessary recovery packages to get the economies back on track (Mennillo 2016). With their rating actions, CRAs contributed decisively to shifting market discourse and drove the redefinition of the crisis: from being a financial crisis to being a sovereign debt crisis in Europe. Consequently, the austerity imperative became the new order of the day to get out of the crisis, and the G20 intentions of 2008 to radically reform the financial system as a lesson from the GFC fell from view.

In the case of corporate ratings, CRAs can reward or punish business practices they find conducive to the company's creditworthiness. This business segment appears as a more straightforward, less controversial or apolitical exercise than the case of rating sovereigns, but it is not. Consider a company that wants to invest in green technologies; it requires the incurring of huge entry costs. This will aggravate the corporate debt situation in the short or medium run, but it will render the institutions more resilient and sustainable in the long run, considering the environmental challenges ahead. Depending on how CRAs take this into account, namely the risks of climate change and ecological collapse in their risk methodologies, ratings will punish or reward those institutions taking precautionary action. In other words, rating can either enforce the status quo or enable change. Against this backdrop, we should be wary of reducing CRAs to a technical component of the infrastructure of global capital markets. CRAs have been, and still are, main drivers behind processes of financialization and key players that govern transnational capital flows. Not least, the impact of authoritative judgements about credit risk has been decisive for the development path of emerging economies, and thus entrenched existing global inequalities.

Why CRAs have become important

How the CRAs' authority has evolved into its current shape is an issue of controversy in scholarly circles. It remains an ongoing debate as to where the true sources of the CRAs' authority lie: whether it is created by the state (state *fiat*); whether it is a market failure arising from the oligopoly; or whether it is the consequence of network externalities (which constitutes a market failure in itself).[5]

As a result of the authority that CRAs have accumulated over the last century, they are sometimes also referred to as the gatekeepers of international bond markets. To put it bluntly, if you are a funding-seeking entity, there is no getting around them in order to gain access to capital. This condition is corroborated by the market concentration, the oligopoly: bond issuers cannot chose between a large variety of agencies to receive a rating; they have to resort to the oligopoly of the Big Three to signal their creditworthiness to investors.

All three agencies are headquartered in the United States (with the exception of Fitch, which maintains dual headquarters in New York and London).[6] Even though the global rating market consists of more than 80 agencies operating either in specific sectors and niche markets or locally, only the Big Three are of global relevance. Market participants, borrowers and lenders all acknowledge their ratings as the authoritative opinions about creditworthiness; the Big Three's ratings matter. Their market share of more than 90 per cent of the world's rating market testifies to the importance of their judgements. Moreover, there are also institutional mechanisms that have supported the market reliance on credit ratings. Regulators use ratings as a tool for credit risk regulation. Institutional investors, such as pension funds, use ratings as investment standards to allocate their clients' savings. These are only a few examples of how far rating has deviated from its original conception as an informed opinion about creditworthiness, which investors can voluntarily take into consideration for their investment decision – or not.

It is tempting to reduce the reason for the oligopoly and the CRAs' authority to institutional reliance and the regulatory use of ratings. It should be mentioned that, compared to the period when the original business idea of ratings was conceived, the reality of today's financial markets is very different. The financial developments since the collapse of the Bretton Woods system have increased the need for credit risk assessments. Over the last 40 years a process often referred to as "financial disintermediation" has involved a transition from a bank-based to a market-based financial system. The banks' "buy and hold" business model has been steadily replaced by "originate and distribute". This implied a reduction in the traditional role of banks in financial intermediation, and an increase in phenomena such as securitization, which allows credit risks to travel.[7] Becoming active market participants themselves, banks gradually delegated their traditional task of due diligence to an independent third party. As a result, the CRAs have become the new intermediaries between those having and those seeking funds. It is worth noting that this type of intermediation is qualitatively different from the financial intermediation that banks have been engaged with traditionally. As the new intermediaries in disintermediated markets, CRAs pass judgements on borrowers without engaging in maturity transformation.[8]

CRAs providing centralized judgements on creditworthiness in disintermediated financial markets may resonate with the idea of CRAs decreasing information asymmetries, as discussed above. To avoid misunderstandings, there is a difference between these two ways of conceptualizing the function of rating. As mentioned earlier, ratings do not convey information that is exempt from interpretation. CRAs provide the dominant interpretation about a debt issuer's creditworthiness, which the majority in the market share and rely on to take investment decisions. Authority is central. CRAs do not discover ratings as if they were an objective figure waiting to be calculated. Ratings are not interchangeable and technical products that can be reproduced by formula, an algorithm or by anyone. They are social constructions of specific trusted companies.

For investors, the process of financial disintermediation has tremendously increased the costs of gathering relevant information to make an assessment about credit risk, as they can no longer rely on banks to scrutinize borrowers. Given that the information overload can be overwhelming and paralysing, ratings represent an extraordinary solution to this problem. Providing centralized judgements, CRAs help investors navigate through the complexity of today's financial markets. They offer a sense of orientation and reduce perceived uncertainty by creating predictability. The CRAs contribute to a stability in the system "that makes political and economic transactions possible" (Abdelal 2009: 73). What is often forgotten is that CRAs can perform this function because there are only a few of them. If there was a multitude of rating suppliers issuing different judgements on borrowers, investors would need to swim through an ocean of rating opinions before taking a decision. From previously scrutinizing borrowers, they would need to assess a multiplicity of rating opinions, potentially increasing the disorientation for investors and driving costs up even further. If rating was about reducing information asymmetries, then more ratings would mean fewer information asymmetries. The opposite is in fact the case, however.[9]

Relating back to the aspect of authority, rating is not just any opinion but an opinion that matters. Performing a signalling function to investors, for borrowers it is crucial that the rating they receive is acknowledged as authoritative in the market. With the increasing complexity of financial markets and the growing amount of data to process, the value added of ratings issued by an authoritative agency even increases. Market participants, above all smaller financial entities, can save immense information costs by relying on the judgement codified in the alphanumeric symbol. Rating is about information processing, abstraction and condensing. The very business idea of rating developed from sorting through large volumes of information and come up with "an easily digested format to investors" (Sinclair 1999: 156). Ratings can thus be regarded as saviours in the data jungle, conferring a sense of increased certainty – not because they reveal more information, but because they provide an assessment, an interpretive framework of existing information.

The CRAs' role in the global financial crisis of 2008

CRAs came to general prominence beyond the financial sector in the wake of the global financial crisis of 2008. Above all for the excessively positive bias of ratings in the lead-up to the crisis, CRAs have come under the spotlight in a way never experienced before in their history. At the peak of the crisis structured financial products with abbreviations such as ABSs and CDOs[10] with top-tier triple-A ratings turned out to be "toxic" assets. CRAs were accused of creating complex models during the housing boom that led to flawed assessments of the default risk of individual mortgages and of the securitized products that contained these mortgages (Council on Foreign Relations 2015). The highly rated structured products were used as collateral on the interbank market – more precisely, in short-term wholesale funding activities. The excessively optimistic ratings contributed to an illusion of safety in the run-up to the financial crisis, allowing the system to "take on far more risk than it could safely handle" (Krugman 2010).

Contagious distrust in the soundness of securitized collateral and in the solvency of borrowing entities led to "dramatic short-term wholesale funding runs" of "cascading, self-reinforcing quality" (Tarullo 2013: 2).[11] This loss in confidence was also reflected in sharp rating downgrades. When housing prices started to collapse in 2007, Moody's downgraded 83 per cent of the "USD 869 billion in mortgage securities" that had been rated triple-A in 2006 (Council on Foreign Relations 2015). In 2010, 93 per cent of formerly triple-A rated subprime-mortgage-backed securities issued in 2006 were given "junk" status, formally known as "non-investment grade" (Krugman 2010).[12]

It has become common practice to identify the rating failure of structured financial products as one of the main causes of the financial crisis. CRAs are accused of having failed to anticipate the end of the housing boom in the United States, reflected in the decline in housing prices, and its effect on loan defaults. Conventional accounts rationalize the cause of the agencies' misjudgement not by doubting the agencies' analytical expertise but by pointing to conflicts of interest related to the agencies' business model of "issuer pays". The agencies' clients were at the same time the issuers of the complex structured products, which created massive conflicts of interest. For reasons of profitability, the agencies would have had an incentive to be more lenient in their assessments in order to please customers and "because of the ongoing threat of losing deals", as stated in one e-mail of a Standard & Poor's (S&P) employee confiscated during investigations by a Senate subcommittee (Krugman 2010). Furthermore, the business segment of structured products was flourishing in the lead-up to the crisis, offering huge growth potential for the rating industry, as the traditional markets of corporate and sovereign ratings had been saturated and mature at the time. In an attempt to attract new market share in the newly booming sector, rating quality would have necessarily suffered. Rating shopping also exacerbated the problem. With the number of competing rating agencies increasing, issuers could choose between a variety of ratings. Unsurprisingly, those agencies bestowing more favourable verdicts preserved market share and attracted more customers than those trying to do an impartial job. That said, the systemic conflicts of interest related to the "issuer pays" business model, with the bargaining power on the side of debt issuers, "corrupted" the rating process (Krugman 2010). Indeed, Moody's accumulated more revenue from structured finance in 2006 – namely $881 million – than all revenues combined for 2001 (*ibid.*). Consequently, a wide consensus emerged that the dominant business model in the rating industry, that the issuer pays, and the conflicts of interest it created were at the heart of the devastating rating failure and, thus, one of the main culprits of the financial crisis.

Credit rating agencies were blamed not only for the excessively optimistic ratings of securitized products but also for their complicity in creating them. CRAs advised their clients how to structure and securitize financial claims on the US subprime mortgage market. Moreover, the auxiliary consultant service comprised direct *ex ante* suggestions on how to modify complex structured financial instruments in order to obtain a better rating. This "cross-selling" of consultancy services has surely exacerbated the conflicts of interest and the upward "issuer pays" rating bias, leading to rating inflation (Amtenbrink & Heine 2013; de Haan & Amtenbrink 2011). So CRAs were first complicit in enhancing the complexity of financial products and thereafter in overrating them (Marandola & Sinclair 2014). These two aspects turned the CRAs into main targets of criticism.

Undoubtedly, the "issuer pays" business model produces conflicts of interest that imply a potential toll on rating quality. In order to make profits, CRAs are under pressure to retain customers and acquire new ones. Consequently, CRAs are deemed to be less rigorous in their assessment of issuers in order to please customers. Trivial though such reasoning may sound, it bears the hallmarks of the toolbox of neoclassical economics, which emphasizes traditional microeconomic problems of incentive structures as drivers of firm behaviour (Dullien 2013). Given the assumption of rent-seeking, the main cause of the experienced rating failure traces back to the problem of "bad incentives" (Bartels & Weder di Mauro 2013).

Scholars studying the politics of rating have pointed out that the presumed rating failure and the distorted incentive structures received too much attention in the aftermath of the crisis, favouring a narrative of apportioning blame to the usual suspects (Sinclair 2010). This has led to a simplistic understanding of the agencies' role, underestimating their constitutive function. Considering how conventional wisdom held that conflicts of interest led to the rating failure in the lead-up to the crisis, it appears even more puzzling that the dominant business model in the rating industry has hitherto remained unchanged.

Current status of the rating agencies: "anything but discredited players"?

"Rating agencies still matter – and that is inexcusable," wrote the famous econo-mist Nouriel Roubini some time after the global financial crisis (Roubini 2015). Despite the harsh criticism and public scrutiny that the CRAs experienced during the GFC, their authoritative status has not been significantly challenged. The way agencies conduct their business, their dominant "issuer pays" business model and the analytics behind ratings have hardly changed. Empirical evidence both in the United States and the European Union suggests that CRAs have not only survived the GFC but are actually thriving.

Figure I.1 shows the total number of credit ratings outstanding reported by the nationally recognized statistical rating organizations (NRSROs) from 2010 to

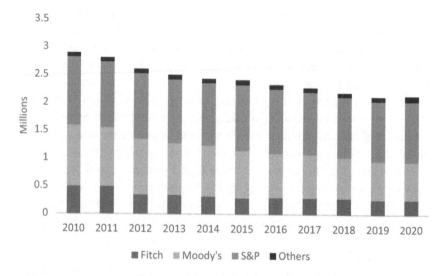

Figure I.1 Total number of credit ratings outstanding across rating categories reported by NRSROs, 2010–20
Source: SEC.

2020 in the United States. The dominance of the Big Three has been persistent over the course of the years following the GFC. Potential competitors were not successful in outstripping the oligopoly.

BOX 1: NRSROs

In the United States, the accreditation of the leading CRAs as "Nationally Recognized Statistical Rating Organizations" (NRSROs) by the Securities and Exchange Commission (SEC) dates back to 1975, with the introduction of rule 15c3-1, also known as the "net capital rule". The rule prioritized bonds that were rated in investment grade – i.e. in the upper half of the rating scale – by at least two NRSROs. If a bond fulfilled this criterion, then investors had to hold less in terms of reserves against it, enjoying a shorter "haircut" or discount. The peculiarity of the net capital rule was that the SEC did not formally specify the eligibility criteria for NRSRO status. The vague NRSRO designation regime gave rise to a puzzling contradiction: although credit ratings were used for regulatory purposes, CRAs themselves were not substantially regulated (Hiss & Nagel 2014: 132). The Credit Rating Agency Reform Act of 2006 established criteria for NRSRO recognition, effectively putting an end to the old and vague NRSRO system. As of this writing, there are nine NRSROs registered with the SEC (listed in alphabetical order):

- A.M. Best Rating Services, Inc.
- DBRS, Inc.
- Egan–Jones Ratings Co. [EJR]
- Fitch Ratings, Inc.
- HR Ratings de México, S.A. de C.V.
- Japan Credit Rating Agency, Ltd [JCR]
- Kroll Bond Rating Agency, Inc. [KBRA]
- Moody's Investors Service, Inc.
- S&P Global Ratings

Source: US Securities and Exchange Commission: www.sec.gov/ocr/ocr-current-nrsros.html.

Looking at the market share distribution from 2018 to 2020 in Figure I.2, you may find it hard to spot the difference – which is exactly the point. Not a lot seems to have changed with regard to the overwhelming dominance of the Big Three. The other NRSROs are providing about 5 per cent of the total of outstanding credit ratings as of 2020.

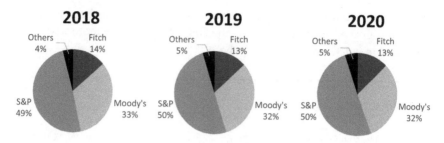

Figure I.2 Market shares by outstanding credit ratings of all NRSROs, 2018–20
Source: SEC.

Table I.1 Percentage by rating category of each NRSRO's outstanding credit ratings of the total outstanding credit ratings of all NRSROs as of 31 December 2020

NRSRO	Financial institutions	Insurance companies	Corporate issuers	Asset-backed securities	Government securities	Total ratings
A. M. Best	N/R	34.1%	0.8%	0.0%	N/R	0.4%
DBRS	7.8%	0.9%	3.4%	15.0%	1.3%	2.9%
EJR	7.1%	4.6%	7.4%	N/R	N/R	1.0%
Fitch	23.4%	15.1%	16.0%	21.8%	10.5%	12.6%
HR Ratings	0.6%	N/R	0.3%	N/R	0.0%	0.1%
JCR	0.7%	0.4%	2.3%	N/R	0.0%	0.2%
KBRA	0.9%	0.6%	0.2%	9.3%	0.0%	0.8%
Moody's	24.1%	12.0%	25.8%	30.3%	33.2%	31.7%
S&P	35.5%	32.2%	43.9%	23.6%	54.9%	50.4%

Note: N/R = not registered.
Source: SEC.

In terms of the rating market per rating category, Table I.1 shows the dominance of the Big Three for ratings of financial institutions, corporate issuers, asset-backed securities and government securities. It is worth noting that S&P issues more than half the total outstanding government security ratings issued by all NRSROs. The only rating category that is not dominated by the Big Three is that of ratings of insurance companies. The market leader for this rating category is the rating agency A.M. Best.

Figure I.3 displays the distribution of outstanding ratings across rating categories and NRSROs. As we can see, 79 per cent, the largest portion of outstanding ratings, are the ratings in the government securities category, which include sovereign ratings and ratings of municipalities. From Table I.1, we can also infer that this is the most concentrated rating category in terms of rating issuance, S&P and Moody's accounting for 88 per cent of all outstanding government ratings (SEC 2022: 26).

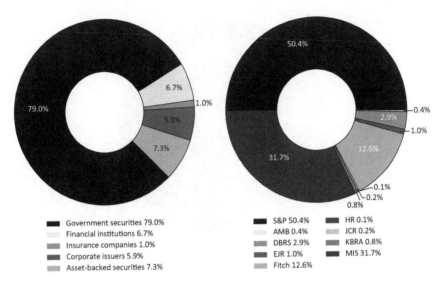

Figure I.3 Distribution of outstanding ratings across rating categories and NRSROs as of December 2020
Source: SEC (2022).

Table I.2 Fiscal year percentage of total reported NRSRO revenue

	2014	*2015*	*2016*	*2017*	*2018*	*2019*	*2020*
Big Three	94.3%	93.7%	94.4%	94.1%	93.5%	93.3%	94.1%
All other NRSROs	5.7%	6.3%	5.6%	5.9%	6.5%	6.7%	5.9%
Total	100.0%	100.0%	100.0%	100.0%	100.0%	100.0%	100.0%

Source: SEC.

Table I.2 shows that the distribution of revenue percentages of total NRSRO revenues since 2014 has also been quite stable. The Big Three account for about 94 per cent in the aggregate, with smaller agencies taking 6 per cent of the revenue percentage per fiscal year (SEC 2022: 29).

As illustrative evidence of what this means in absolute numbers: NRSROs reported $7.1 billion as total revenue for the 2017 fiscal year (1 October to 30 September). The revenue reported to the SEC in 2016 was approximately $5.9 billion. This shows that the industry is dynamic and striving despite the rating debacle experienced during the GFC.

If we look at the data in the European Union, the situation does not differ significantly from that in the United States (see Figure I.4). Taking into account the agencies' turnover generated from credit rating activities and ancillary services in the European Union, the Big Three can account for approximately 92 per cent of market share (European Securities and Markets Authority [ESMA] 2021).

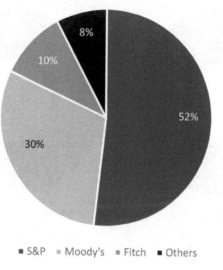

■ S&P   ■ Moody's   ■ Fitch   ■ Others

Figure I.4 Market share of CRAs in the European Union
Source: ESMA (2021).

Table I.3 Rank of Big Three per asset class

Asset class	S&P	Moody's	Fitch
Structured finance instruments	3	1	2
Non-financial corporates*	1	2	3
Financial corporates	2	1	3
Insurance undertakings*	1	2	3
Sovereigns and public entities*	1	3	2

Source: ESMA (2021).
* The ranking holds for solicited ratings.

Likewise, we can observe a persistent dominance of the Big Three per asset class in the European Union (ESMA 2021: 8–10). S&P, Moody's and Fitch lead by a wide margin, even though in different order depending on the rating category (see Table I.3). For example, for ratings of structured finance instruments Moody's spearheads the market, with Fitch coming second and S&P third.

The resilience of CRAs

At first sight, it appears paradoxical that the agencies' reputation in the aftermath of the GFC has not suffered but, instead, proved to be resilient. As I discuss in this book, this is not a puzzle but a common pattern when it comes to the relationship between CRAs and crises. CRAs have succeeded in retaining their authority after a series of seemingly existential crises. Instead of irreversibly damaging the CRAs' reputation, as one might expect, CRAs used, for example, the Enron debacle and the GFC a few years later to their advantage, their failures and mistakes notwithstanding. Indulging in the values that are cherished by the market empowered the CRAs to credibly signal that they are able to learn.

In the case of Enron, there were demands to speed up the rating process, which led to a paradigm shift to high-frequency rating. The Enron case was constructed as a problem of missing information and of the process being too slow. During the 1980s (Sinclair 2005: 172) "[g]reater international capital mobility has brought greater volatility to markets and greater problems in assigning ratings and adjusting them in a timely fashion that meets the concerns of investors and other parties". As CRAs are supposed to "know better", they were especially vulnerable to attack. In an effort to "dispel an image of complacency" when under attack (*ibid.*: 169), CRAs legitimized themselves by becoming faster and more efficient. Likewise, in the case of the GFC, CRAs put serious effort into increasing their transparency, constantly updating and publishing their rating methodologies on their websites. The more conservative assessments of sovereign debt in the context of the European sovereign debt crisis in the wake of the GFC and the Asian financial crisis of 1997–99 can also be read as the CRAs' attempt to compensate for past mistakes, demonstrate their learning capability and restore credibility (Ferri, Liu & Stiglitz 1999).

In the case of the Asian financial crisis, "rating agencies attached higher weights to their qualitative judgement than they gave to the economic fundamentals" (*ibid.*: 349). History repeated itself in the course of the European sovereign debt crisis, when CRAs faced criticism for having downgraded countries after 2008 more severely than was apparently warranted by economic fundamentals (Fuchs & Gehring 2017; Gärtner & Griesbach 2012; Gärtner, Griesbach & Jung 2011). Again, the so-called qualitative component accounted for the conservative ratings (Hiss & Nagel 2014). According to Bruner and Abdelal (2005: 194–5), the CRAs "have depended, perhaps paradoxically, on some instability in sovereign bond markets: Crises and defaults increase the potential value to investors of the agencies' expertise at the same time that they threaten to dry up the market or expose agencies to criticism." The different crises that CRAs experienced in their history meant a reputational exposure, but, most importantly, they offered the agencies an opportunity to distinguish themselves. Whether it was the GFC, the European sovereign debt crisis, Enron or the Asian financial crisis, CRAs seized the opportunity to their advantage. In all these cases, the market accepted the agencies' reactions to these crises as signals that the CRAs' (epistemic) authority was still intact.

Overview of the book

The next chapter discusses the definition of rating and the conceptualization of CRAs as a case of structural power in the global economy. It also introduces the main companies of the CRA industry, which are of global relevance: the three largest credit rating agencies, also known as the "Big Three": Standard & Poor's Global Ratings, Moody's Investors Service and Fitch Ratings. As elaborated earlier, smaller agencies account only for a low level of market share in the industry, usually being specialized in one sector or country, such as A.M. Best in the US insurance sector, or the Toronto-headquartered DBRS Morningstar[13] for structured finance instruments in the European Union.

I also look into the historical origins of the CRAs, going back to the middle of the nineteenth century, and how the industry has transformed over the centuries. For example, I find that there are increasing similarities between rating and the media industry today. Moreover, we learn about the transition from the "investor pays" business model to the "issuer pays" model. As a result of developments in information and communication technology (ICT), "issuer pays" has become the dominant business model in the rating industry. Chapter 2 analyses what credit rating agencies do. It examines the rating scale, the habitual market division of the rating scale into investment grade and non-investment grade, and the rating methodologies for the various rating types; sovereign, sub-sovereign and corporate. Chapter 3 enquires into the use of ratings in order to understand the purposes that ratings fulfil in today's financial markets.

Chapter 4 provides an overview of the variety of "CRA critique". I examine conventional accounts of CRA criticism, such as conflicts of interest, US home bias, the lack of competition and the timeliness of ratings. Thereby, I unveil important aspects about the CRAs' authority, which are often overlooked. Furthermore, the chapter discusses the fruitful relationship between the CRA critique and the CRAs' authority, which lies at the heart of the CRAs' crisis resilience. Chapter 5 highlights the regulatory responses that policy-makers have come up with to get a grip on the challenges that credit rating agencies pose to global financial markets and economies worldwide, looking at the United States, transnational efforts and the European Union. Chapter 6 presents the status of credit rating in China. After a brief history and an overview of the major players, a discussion follows on the rating market's dysfunctionalities and the attempt to liberalize, allowing the Big Three to run fully operational units on the mainland. The book ends with a conclusion providing an outlook of the potential developments impacting the rating industry and the major challenges ahead.

1

THE "WHAT" AND THE "WHO" ABOUT CREDIT RATING

What is a rating and what is it not?

Ratings are conventionally, and erroneously, regarded as metrics about the probability of default of a debt issuer. Ratings are not the product of calculation, however. In fact, rating is a judgement on a debt issuer's prospect of repayment of the liability on time and in full. Legally speaking, a rating is not an investment recommendation. In line with the rating industry's original business idea, a rating offers an opinion about the creditworthiness of a financial product. Investors may consider this opinion before taking their investment decisions, but a rating does not exempt investors from due diligence. This distinction is highly relevant, as it protects credit rating agencies from liability claims by virtue of the first amendment of the US constitution, which guarantees freedom of speech and of the press, among other things. According to Moody's Investors Service (2013b: 4), credit ratings are "forward-looking opinions of the relative credit risks of financial obligations issued by non-financial corporates, financial institutions, structured finance vehicles, project finance vehicles, and public sector entities". According to the website of S&P Global Ratings, a credit rating is best described as an "informed opinion",[1] conveying the impression of an underlying well-thought-out process instead of an ad hoc, spontaneous whim:

> Credit ratings are forward looking opinions about an issuer's relative creditworthiness. They provide a common and transparent global language for investors to form a view on and compare the relative likelihood of whether an issuer may repay its debts on time and in full. Credit ratings are just one of many inputs that investors and other market participants can consider as part of their decision-making processes.

From these official definitions of credit rating, we can make a few observations: First, the two major CRAs concur in defining ratings as "forward-looking opinions". The word "judgement" does not appear. There is an emphasis on ratings being *relative* in two ways: first, because of the ordinal scale, ratings are supposed to be relative measures of credit risk in comparison to each other; and, second, ratings should be used as one input among many to assess creditworthiness, which suggests that the CRAs reject claims of absoluteness. At the same time, CRAs claim authorship for the common language of credit risk. Therefore, the implication is that ratings are *constitutive of* creditworthiness; creditworthiness has come to mean "credit rating". Finally – as if CRAs were aware of the tensions between defining rating as opinion and stylizing it as a technical product – they do not refer to credit ratings explicitly in terms of "probability" of default but, rather, of "likelihood". Unlike the former, "likelihood" does not necessarily imply that the rating is a metric, but it does not explicitly exclude it either.[2]

To a certain extent, the easy-to-understand alphanumerical rating symbol conveys the impression of objectively calculated probabilities. Instead of using cumbersome text to reproduce what a rating actually is declared to be, namely an "informed opinion", the conversion into the letter grade facilitates the appearance as a quasi-scientific relative measure of credit risk. The rating symbol helps ratings pretend to be something they are not, inducing market participants to believe that ratings are unambiguous figures. As if the rating users desire a reality that can be captured in a probability distribution, the symbol offers a pleasant fallacy of precision, assuming a law-like repeatability of history, while assuming away contingencies of social reality.

Why does this distinction between what a rating actually is in legal terms and what it is commonly thought (and wished) to be matter? It has something to do with the CRAs' authority. CRAs benefit if ratings are perceived as probabilities of default. A "positivist" aura makes ratings appear objective.[3] CRAs gain in credibility if ratings are regarded as metrics. Therefore, it is not surprising that CRAs do not explicitly reject the notion of ratings being a technical product. The perception of ratings as measured probabilities of default amounts to a farce as it suggests a positivist epistemology without entirely following it. Sinclair (2005: 46) maintains that "agencies assert that rating determinations are opinions but simultaneously seek to objectify and offer their views as facts". Thus CRAs face a continuous dilemma that demands a delicate balancing act from them. In turn, to equate an opinion with a technical product takes courage, and confirms the CRAs' self-conception of their authoritative status. Market participants' tacit tolerance of this tension only testifies to this.

The authority of CRAs – and, related to it, the popularity of ratings – cannot be explained without taking into account firmly held beliefs about the possibilities of how we can know about the future. This *epistemological* aspect is crucial for understanding the agencies' success. The very "existence of rating agencies necessarily assumes predictability" (Sinclair 1999: 164). The rating symbol invokes predictability, and, with that, the assumption that the future is knowable and can be anticipated. This is independent of the number of cases of default that are used as a basis for their assessments. In other words, the impression that the future is predictable is conveyed both with "small" and with "large" n (i.e. cases of default). The rating symbol does so without resorting to stochastic measurements, regardless of whether these calculations are even feasible.[4] The question as to whether prediction is possible at all is irrelevant in the case of CRAs. What matters is that the rating format gives a pretence of predictability and computability, and market participants buy into it.

Paradoxically, the more ratings pretend to be something they are not, the more credible they become. By portraying their ratings as metrics and products of stochastic calculations, not only do CRAs become accomplices to scientistic approaches but their ratings gain legitimization. The more credibly the impression of stochastic calculations based on "hard facts" is conveyed, the more the judgemental, inconclusive character of the creditworthiness assessment is glossed over. This is why, within certain boundaries, it is not surprising that CRAs vow to stick to a scientistic methodology in their official communications. For example, Fitch states in the case of sovereign ratings (Fitch Ratings 2002: 3–4):

> It is important, though, that investors realise the limitations of this exercise, which is necessarily far less certain than our ability to analyse either bank or corporate risks of default. The essential problem is that the world of sovereign borrowers is far smaller than the world of large banks or corporations, and that the number of instances of default in the modern period when we have reasonable national accounts is tinier still. [...] So the rating of sovereigns depends more on the art of political economy than on the science of econometrics.

The Fitch warning suggests that, if there were sufficient n, an indication of the probability of sovereign default would be based more on econometric calculations; the opinion, would become, so to speak, less opinion, and more scientific. Against the background that the proportion of the admixture of quantitative and qualitative data as well as interpretive elements remains unknown, the differentiation regarding whether the rating judgement is based on the art of political economy or the science of econometrics is actually obsolete, whether with small or large n. Further, the rating symbol conveys the impression of calculated predictability and comparability either way.

Fitch's statement can be understood as a concession regarding the limits of the positivist stance that CRAs usually adopt to be credible and, at the same time, as an invocation thereof. The inadequacy of calculation in the special case of sovereign ratings is attributed to the "not enough n problem", and not to its inherently judgemental nature. The irony in all this is that, even if there *were* enough cases of default, a rating would not amount to a measure of probability of default. If rating was a repeatable algorithm then there would not be a business case for having CRA ratings, as everyone could reproduce them. But ratings make a difference, as they "price in the priceless".[5]

A common understanding *limits* the agencies' role to one of an informational intermediary that decreases the information asymmetries between investors and borrowers. From such a perspective, a rating is a suitable problem-solving device that coordinates actions "between those having funds to invest and those seeking funds to use" (Sinclair 1999: 164). In comparison to when ratings were invented at the beginning of the twentieth century, and given the increase in information asymmetries, today's market-based finance has increased the demand for information about credit risk and, thus, for ratings.[6] Unsurprisingly, and in line with conventional wisdom, CRAs portray themselves in such a functionalist perspective in their self-representation. They see the usefulness of ratings as decreasing market inefficiencies, which is just an alternative expression for reducing information asymmetries: "Credit ratings help facilitate an efficient capital marketplace. They provide transparent third-party information that's not only forward-looking, but standardized for consistency."[7]

In a functionalist perspective, information about credit risk is seen as neutral, objective and measurable, and thus as unambiguous, with no room for interpretation. Even though this is seldom spelled out, this implies that the agencies' work is assumed as replaceable and multipliable. CRA ratings are seen as independent, third-party opinions about credit risk. Since borrowers would be incentivized to downplay the riskiness of their projects, whereas those having funds – the investors – would have an incentive to overestimate these risks, the idea is that CRAs minimize the bias in reporting credit risks. In the ideal case, CRAs have the key role of balancing the distorted perceptions of credit risk between the two parties in order to provide a supposedly neutral assessment of the debt issuers' creditworthiness.[8]

The acknowledgement of the authoritative standing of only a few agencies whose ratings matter challenges such a reading. Ratings are not reproducible technical metrics that can be issued by any entity. When issuing ratings, CRAs provide centralized interpretations of creditworthiness that are commonly shared between market participants. This is why questions of authority and rating are inextricably linked. Ratings provide orientation for a multitude of actors in disintermediated markets. An unlimited number of rating agencies intermediating between borrowers and lenders, as assumed in a functionalist perspective, would undermine this guiding function of rating.

The centralized, dominant interpretations of creditworthiness that CRAs provide do not emerge from nothing. Rating is based on knowledge that is intersubjectively shared and validated among the finance and business communities. A rating is an aggregated social judgement. For example, sovereign ratings shape and reproduce the common sense, the market orthodoxy, the norms and dominant ideas about fiscal and economic policy. From these observations we can draw two implications in terms of the relevance of CRAs that go beyond a conventional functionalist reading of rating. First, in order to establish whether CRAs matter, it is to no avail to frame the question as "Who follows whom?": the market following the CRAs or the other way round. This is attributable to the inherently intersubjective nature of the rating business. Much scholarly effort went into analysing empirical evidence as to whether markets "really follow" the CRAs. Trivial though it sounds, whether ratings have an effect on the market's creditworthiness perception of bond issuers – "interest rates", as economists would say, or "yields", as practitioners say – is difficult to grasp in econometric terms (this often holds true for econometrics, and causality in general). Because of this measurement problem, the claim that CRAs "matter" lacks robust evidence. Ratings are imputed to have no independent influence on interest rates, resulting in a tenaciously held mantra that ratings would "only follow the markets", and, by extension, that CRAs would not matter. Taking intersubjectivity into account, we can decouple the discussion about the CRAs' authority from the "Who follows whom?" question, and glean important insights into the very nature of the agencies' role in today's financialized capitalism.

Second, as a consequence of the agencies' authority – more precisely, epistemic authority (CRAs define the relevant knowledge about creditworthiness) – ratings are even constitutive of creditworthiness. Creditworthiness is defined by ratings; "creditworthiness" has come to mean, and boils down to, "credit rating". Illustrative evidence for this bold claim can be found, for example, in the Free Dictionary. The online dictionary and encyclopaedia paraphrases the adjective "creditworthy" as having an "acceptable" or "satisfactory" credit rating.[9] CRAs have gained power of definition over creditworthiness: a bond issuer is deemed creditworthy *because* it has the top rating, rather than the top rating reflecting a preconceived notion of creditworthiness. As CRAs invented and can claim authorship of the common language of credit risk on financial markets, this legitimizes and testifies to their position as epistemic authority. At the same time, thanks to their position as epistemic authority, they enjoy the credibility and reputation to continue to provide the common language of risk – several crises notwithstanding.

CRAs as a case of structural power

The authority of CRAs can be conceptualized by, for example, drawing on Strange's structural power (Mennillo 2016). Strange (1998: 24–5) defines structural power as "the power to shape and determine the structures of the global political economy within which other states, their political institutions, their economic enterprises and (not least) their scientists and other professional people have to operate". Structural power confers the authority to the relevant players in the global political economy to decide how things shall be done. Those institutions exerting structural power can change the range of choices by, for instance, imposing costs. In the case of ratings, CRAs can define the terms and conditions under which a country, a company or a municipality can have access to credit. This often occurs without pressurizing others directly into taking a specific decision rather than another. Structural power is less visible and tangible, more subtle than relational power narrowly understood. Regarding the subtle quality of structural power in the case of CRAs, Sinclair (1999: 165) states that

> an important feature of … bond-rating agencies is their epistemic authority and closely related structural power, rather than direct "power wielding." The reason for this is that authority and structural power are built upon a certain base of consent. This is a more robust structure upon which the social forces associated with coordination can generate legitimacy for their view of the world, for their approach to problems and their distribution of payoffs to allied social interests.

Structural power analysis does not focus on the CRAs' individual motivations, intentions or vested interests of different rating actions. For this reason, "[e]pistemic authority and structural power are … much harder to specify than the variables international political economist are used to. Not only is authority seemingly more intangible, it is also constantly being both constructed and worn away" (*ibid.*).

Strange's concept of structural power consists of the idea that its origins are diffused across four structures: the control over security, over production, over credit (finance) and over knowledge, beliefs and ideas. The four structures indicate where social power relations are at play and suggest the cause of these power relations. The interactions between the four separate but related structures lead to a high diffusion of the effects of the respective power structures (Strange 1998: 26). In the specific case of CRAs, structural power in the form of "knowledge, beliefs and ideas" is exerted within the finance structure: a case of interweaving structural power sources. This specific conjuncture of the two structural power sources suggests that the effects of such kind of power are highly diffused. It explains why CRAs are an epistemic authority not only in finance but also in the public discourse on sovereign creditworthiness. Moreover, it suggests why the sovereign rating practice can shape shared understandings, norms and beliefs about a state's creditworthiness, and, implicitly, about fiscal and economic policy. At the same time, the finance structure, the CRAs' control over access to credit and their role as the market's gatekeepers, provides the monetary leverage that allows the epistemic authority to materialize, thus enabling the perception inherent in the sovereign rating assessment to shape the reality it pretends to describe without interacting with the object of assessment. Thus it is that, according to Sinclair (1999: 161–2), "through a process of consent-generation and coercion", CRAs coordinate creditors' and debtors' perceptions "to a certain well-understood or transparent set that is shared among themselves". What is regarded as acceptable by the CRAs "is reflected in the minds of capital-market participants". This codification "is a reflection of the structural power of the agencies, the anticipation of the agencies' views by others and their action to meet these anticipated judgements". As a result, CRAs "shape the internal organization and behaviour of those institutions seeking funds" in anticipation.

The Big Three

The following company profiles of the Big Three are certainly not exhaustive, but they summarize the most salient details to build a picture of the CRAs and the industry. The profiles contain essentials about each company's ownership and structure, financials, staff and products, as well as their historical origins.

Standard & Poor's Global Ratings

Standard & Poor's Global Ratings ("S&P") was founded in 1888 and is headquartered in New York. S&P is owned by the eponymous publicly listed S&P Global, Inc. Its three largest stockholders are the Vanguard Group, SSgA Funds Management and BlackRock Fund Advisors.[10] Remarkably, these three asset management companies are the same asset managers that dominate the global exchange-traded fund (ETF) market, having a combined market share of 80 per cent: BlackRock (39 per cent), Vanguard (25 per cent) and SSgA (16 per cent).[11] In addition to ratings, S&P Global operates two other business segments, namely market and commodities intelligence, and indices.

According to its self-image, S&P's "globally respected credit ratings paired with unparalleled thought leadership ... empower people to make informed, confident decisions":[12]

> [S&P Global] Ratings is an independent provider of credit ratings, research and analytics to investors, issuers and other market participants. Credit ratings are one of several tools investors can use when making

decisions about purchasing bonds and other fixed income investments. They are opinions about credit risk and our ratings express our opinion about the ability and willingness of an issuer, such as a corporation or state or city government, to meet its financial obligations in full and on time. Our credit ratings can also relate to the credit quality of an individual debt issue, such as a corporate or municipal bond, and the relative likelihood that the issue may default.[13]

The market and commodities intelligence services of S&P provide auxiliary tools for the financial community and corporations. Services include the tracking of performance; help to generate better investment returns, identify new trading and investment ideas; performing risk analysis; the development of mitigation strategies; and providing high-value information to the commodity and energy markets.[14] The indices segment of S&P Global maintains an array of stock indices, including the prominent S&P 500 and the Dow Jones Industrial Average.[15] Compared to the other two rating agencies among the Big Three, this puts S&P in a unique position in financial markets as a transnational epistemic authority.

In 2017 the revenue of S&P's Global Ratings was almost $3 billion, representing nearly half the total revenue of S&P Global.[16] The market and commodities intelligence division generated revenue of $2.5 billion[17] and the indices division $733 million.[18] Over a period of six years S&P managed to increase its revenue by two-thirds. In 2011 the agency's revenue had amounted only to $1.77 billion, of which 52 per cent was generated in the United States and 48 per cent internationally. Profits amounted to $719 million. It would be fair to say that S&P survived the 2008 global financial crisis successfully.

In 2019 S&P Global employed approximately 23,000 people. The rating agency employs about 1,500 credit analysts.[19] In total, the company has more than 1 million credit ratings outstanding.[20] It operates in seven sectors depending on the type of debt issuer: corporations, financial institutions, governments, infrastructure and utilities, insurance, structured finance and US public finance. Figure 1.1 shows the outstanding ratings of S&P per rating category reported to the SEC as of 31 December 2020.

As the name implies, today's S&P is the legacy of a merger between two firms: Poor's Publishing Company and Standard Statistics Company. This merger took place in 1941 and constitutes the birth of the Standard & Poor's Corporation. The parent companies of S&P and the historical origins of debt security rating date back to the middle of the nineteenth century. Originally fuelled by the "public controversy and market turbulence created by failed railroads, dubious Florida land schemes, and other property deals in the newly opened lands of the western United States" (Sinclair 2005: 23), US financial markets had already experienced "an information explosion" in the years

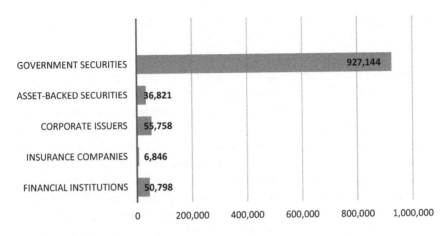

Figure 1.1 Outstanding ratings, S&P Global
Source: SEC (2022).

before the First World War. *Poor's American Railroad Journal* of the mid-1850s preceded the *History of the Railroads and Canals of the United States*, which Henry Varnum Poor published in 1860.[21] The book contained detailed information about the track length of railroads and investors' share capital, and a record of the railroads' profit and loss. Having founded the H. V. & H. W. Poor Company, Henry Varnum Poor (1812–1905) and his son Henry William Poor (1844–1915) launched *Poor's Manual of the Railroads of the United States* in 1868: within a few months, "they sell all 2,500 copies of the first issue. Each copy, at 442 pages, is priced $5 and contains essential information for investors in the US railroad industry. The *Manual* is updated annually, keeping investors current and allowing them to chart a company's progress over the years."[22] The manual enjoyed great popularity, as is evidenced by the 5,000 subscribers in early 1880 (Kirkland 1961: 233). In 1899 the company was renamed after Henry Varnum Poor's son Henry William and became H. W. Poor & Company. At some point after 1908, the year in which it became public that Henry William Poor's mergers in the colonial sugar industry and various railway companies had not succeeded (*New York Times* 1908), the successor company, Poor's Railroad Manual Company, was founded.[23] It issued its first rating in 1916 (Sinclair 2005: 24).

In 1919 Poor's Railroad Manual Company merged with Moody's Manual Company to form Poor's Publishing Company. This merger intertwined the origins of Moody's and Standard and Poor's, giving rise to considerable confusion in the aftermath. Moody's Manual Company had formerly been known as John Moody & Company, which was sold by John Moody in the wake of the stock market crash of 1907 and is not to be confused with Moody's Investors

Service, which came into existence in 1913. In 1914 Roy Ward Porter had acquired Moody's Manual Company after having worked as its editor since 1908. As a result of the 1919 merger between Poor's Railroad Manual Company and Moody's Manual Company, the rival company of the then already existing Moody's Investors Service had the legal right to use the "Moody's" name until 1925, when "Moody's bought back the rights to use the name exclusively for $100,000" (Sinclair 2005: 25). In this context, Sinclair (*ibid.*) notes that "the complicated lineage of what we know today as Moody's and S&P has rarely been mentioned in print and seems little known among rating agency staff".[24]

Standard Statistics Bureau was founded by Luther Lee Blake (1874–1953) in 1906. Having bought the Stock and Bond Card System from Roger Babson in 1913, the Standard Statistics Bureau was incorporated as Standard Statistics Incorporation in 1914. The Babson Stock and Bond Card System had published financial reports on stocks and bonds, similar to cards published by Standard Statistics. Between 1922 and 1923 Standard Statistics Incorporation started to rate corporate bonds and municipal securities.[25] In 1941 the merger with Poor's Publishing Company took place, forming Standard & Poor's Corporation.

In 1964 McGraw-Hill Publishing Company and McGraw-Hill Book Company merged to form McGraw-Hill, Inc. Then in 1966, McGraw-Hill, Inc. bought Standard and Poor's Corporation. In 2013 McGraw-Hill changed its corporate name to McGraw-Hill Financial. In addition to Standard and Poor's Ratings Services, other subsidiaries of McGraw-Hill Financial at the time were S&P Capital IQ, S&P Dow Jones Indices, and Platts and J.D. Power. In 2016 McGraw-Hill Financial changed its name to S&P Global Inc. This was significant, as all subsidiaries of S&P Global Inc. were rebranded to "S&P" to reflect the more familiar brand name, which is globally known and conducive to a coherent corporate identity.

Moody's Investors Service

Moody's Investors Service ("Moody's") was founded in 1909 and is headquartered in New York. Since 1998 the rating agency has been owned by the eponymous Moody's Corporation, which is listed on the New York Stock Exchange (NYSE). The largest stockholders are Berkshire Hathaway, the Vanguard Group and BlackRock Fund Advisors,[26] the latter two also being shareholders in S&P Global (as mentioned above, this is not the only commonality between Moody's and S&P). In addition to the credit rating agency Moody's Investors Service, Moody's Corporation also owns a second business segment, Moody's Analytics. Moody's publishes ratings globally, and revenue is mainly generated by the debt issuers, who mandate Moody's to produce ratings to facilitate the distribution of their debt issues to investors.[27] In contrast, the Moody's Analytics segment offers a wide range of products and services in the area of financial analysis and risk management in terms of institutional participants in global financial markets. It also serves as provider of business intelligence and company information.[28]

In the wake of the GFC, in 2011 Moody's Investors Service generated revenue of $1.569 billion, of which 56 per cent originated in the United States and 44 per cent internationally. Profits amounted to $690 million, despite the fact that the company came under fire during this period in the media and the public. Regardless of the criticism the industry faced in view of its involvement in the subprime crisis and its pivotal role in the European sovereign debt crisis, over the years the revenues of Moody's Corporation have continued to thrive. In 2013 the revenue generated was $2.97 billion. In 2017 the revenue of the credit rating agency Moody's Investors Service was $2.89 billion, nearly 70 per cent of Moody's Corporation's total revenue.[29] Compared to the previous year, it had increased by 17 per cent. The revenue of the Moody's Analytics segment in 2017 was $1.45 billion, 16 per cent more than in 2016.[30]

Moody's Investors Service employs almost 12,000 staff members, with 30 per cent located in the United States and the other 70 per cent in international offices operating in 40 countries worldwide.[31] Moody's Investors Service provides ratings in more than 120 countries. Rated entities were as of 31 December 2017:[32]

- non-financial corporate issuers (4,700);
- financial institutions issuers (4,100);
- public finance issuers (18,000), including sovereign, sub-sovereign and supranational issuers;
- structured finance transactions (11,000);
- infrastructure and project finance issuers (1,000).

As with S&P, the history of Moody's dates back to the early days of the twentieth century. John Moody and Company, the predecessor institution of the rating agency, was founded in 1900. Its first publication was *Moody's Manual of Industrial and Miscellaneous Securities*. General information on the railroads was available at the time, but there was a lack of "useful data on the emerging industrial combinations" (Sinclair 2005: 23). John Moody's business idea was born:

> The manual provided information and statistics on stocks and bonds of financial institutions, government agencies, manufacturing, mining, utilities, and food companies. Within two months the publication had sold out. By 1903, circulation had exploded, and Moody's Manual was known from coast to coast.[33]

The stock market crash of 1907 forced John Moody to sell "John Moody & Company" (*ibid.*: 24). This sale of the manual business linked the histories between the two rivals, Moody's and S&P. In 1909 John Moody came up with a new business idea and he published *Moody's Analyses of Railroad Investments*. Compared with the competitors' timing, be it of Poor's Railroad Manual Company or of Standard Statistics Company, Moody's Analyses Publishing Company became the first *to rate* public market securities.

> [I]nstead of simply collecting information on the property, capital-ization, and management of companies, he now offered investors an analysis of security values. His company would publish a book that analyzed the railroads and their outstanding securities. It offered concise conclusions about their relative investment quality. [...] [It] described for readers the analytic principles that Moody used to assess a railroad's operations, management, and finance.[34]

Even though John Moody was the first mover in the rating industry in terms of execution, it would be erroneous to claim that this was his innovation (*ibid.*). Two young men, Roger Babson and Freeman Putney, Jr, "during or before 1901 ... conceived the idea of security ratings" on their manifold travels by rail to Boston, the then financial centre of New England (Harold 1938: 9):

> [F]or years [they had] been interested in investment securities, their quotations, and financial statistics. The rapid growth of the market and the glamorous possibilities of financial captaincies gripped their imaginations. [...] It was not, however, until 1909 that security ratings were published on a scale large enough to be called to public attention, and it was done neither by Mr. Babson nor Mr. Putney.

It was done by John Moody. Going beyond pure description, Moody's Analyses Publishing Company expressed conclusions based, as the name implies, on an analysis of the stocks and bonds of the US railroads. Moody went from providing compendiums of information about investment possibilities to actually making judgements about the creditworthiness of debtors, using the letter grades as the rating symbol. This form of representation was also not a completely new idea. It was adopted from the mercantile credit rating of retail businesses and wholesalers that had already been in existence since the late nineteenth cen-tury.[35] The unique selling point of credit rating was to select and consolidate all the existing information deemed relevant to a debt issuer's creditworthiness, leading to a "focal point" for investors in the guise of an alphanumeric symbol (Boot, Milbourn & Schmeits 2006).

In 1913 the company name was changed to Moody's Investors Service. This new label reflected more accurately the expansion of the base of analysed companies to industrial companies and utilities. The next year Moody's Investors Service was incorporated. At that time it had already started expanding the "rating coverage to bonds issued by US cities and other municipalities. By 1924, Moody's ratings covered nearly 100 per cent of the US bond market."[36]

Fitch Ratings

Fitch Ratings Inc. ("Fitch") was founded in 1914, and it is the only rating agency of the Big Three that is headquartered in both New York and London. As the smallest player of the Big Three, Fitch has succeeded in becoming the world's third largest rating agency through its eventful history of mergers and acquisitions.

Since April 2018 Fitch Group has been fully owned by the Hearst Corporation, which is a mass media and business intelligence conglomerate (*Financial Times* 2018a). Fitch is Hearst's largest wholly owned company (Hearst 2019). Hearst describes Fitch Group as a "credit ratings and financial data company", distinguishing itself as more than a credit rating agency (*ibid.*). Hearst Corporation includes other holdings, such as *The Oprah Magazine*, *Good Housekeeping*, *Cosmopolitan* and numerous television stations and newspapers. Constituent parts of the Fitch Group are Fitch Ratings (including Fitch Bohua, which has operated in mainland China since May 2020); Fitch Learning, which offers financial training and professional development; Fitch Solutions, which is a provider of credit market data, analytical tools and risk services; and Fitch Ventures, which invests in early-stage financial information, service and technology companies.[37]

Since Hearst's takeover in 2018, Fitch's financial reporting has been fully managed by its parent company. Hearst's total revenue for 2018 was $11.4 billion (Hearst 2019). When Hearst purchased the 20 per cent stake in Fitch from Fimalac in 2018, 20 per cent of Fitch's revenue derived from products unrelated to the core rating business (*Financial Times* 2018a). No further revenue information about Fitch is available, as Hearst is not a public company, and no annual report is published. According to the *2016 Annual Report* published by Fimalac SA, a French holding company which had previously owned 20 per cent stake in Fitch until 2018, Fitch's revenue was $1.17 billion (Fimalac 2016: 9). Revenue derived from ratings services constituted slightly over 70 per cent of Fitch Group's total revenue in the same year, with the remaining derived from the other business segments, such as Fitch Solutions (research and subscriptions), Fitch Learning (learning and training), Business Monitor International[38] and other streams.[39]

Fitch Ratings has 38 global offices and employs more than 2,000 analysts worldwide. It rates over 20,000 entities, covering corporates, public finance, sovereigns, structured finance, insurance, etc. The background to the dual headquarter situation, in London and New York, relates back to the history of Fitch. In 1992 Fimalac acquired IBCA (International Bank Credit Analysts). IBCA was a small London-based agency with 38 employees, with a good reputation in European bank ratings. At the time this was regarded as "the first step toward the creation of a true European rating agency", given that both S&P's and Moody's were North American (Sinclair 2005: 29; see also Bruce 1992). Having gradually "built an international network of offices, mainly in continental Europe but also in South America", IBCA, headquartered in London, was generating revenues of over $30 million by the end of 1997 and employed approximately 180 employees.[40] In order to grow further and to achieve a global market presence, access to the world's largest rating market, the US financial market, was inevitable. The regulatory measures of the SEC prevented IBCA from rating US issuers, however: IBCA did not appear on the list of nationally recognized statistical rating organizations, which is a precondition for operating in the United States. The idea of establishing a purely European CRA of global relevance had to be abandoned within less than a decade after Fimalac's investment in IBCA. In 1997 Fimalac bought US-based Fitch Ratings, which was then merged with UK-based IBCA (Fimalac 2016: 8), forming Fitch-IBCA, with headquarters in both New York and London.

The history of US-based Fitch dates back to the beginnings of the twentieth century. John Knowles Fitch founded the Fitch Publishing Company in New York City on 24 December 1913. Having published "security quotations" and financial statistics, the company issued the first ratings in 1924, which were initially limited to bonds, but afterward also included stock ratings (Harold 1938: 13–14). After the merger between IBCA and Fitch, the number of employees grew to 750, and the revenues increased from $156 million in 1998 to $172 million in 1999.[41] Fimalac's strategic goal was "to raise Fitch-IBCA to a position alongside Moody's and Standard & Poor's, the two US-based agencies that dominated the global market".[42] In 2000 two acquisitions were critical to the realization of this goal. In April Fimalac successfully took over the Chicago-based Duff & Phelps Credit Rating Company (D&P), the fourth largest rating agency at the time. It was then merged with Fitch-IBCA, to become Fitch-IBCA Duff & Phelps. Then, in December, Thomson Financial Services sold its subsidiary, the Canada-based BankWatch, to Fimalac. Consequently, Fitch-IBCA Duff & Phelps was rebranded as Fitch Ratings.

In 2006 Hearst bought its first 20 per cent minority stake from Fimalac for $592 million (*Financial Times* 2018a). In 2009 Fimalac sold a further 20 per cent stake to Hearst for $427 million (Reuters 2009). In the meantime, Fitch was employing 1,049 analysts at the end of 2010. In 2011 its revenue amounted to $733 million, of which 39 per cent was generated in the United States and the rest internationally, and profits were $227 million. In 2012 Hearst bought another 10 per cent for $177 million, resulting in Fimalac and Hearst each owning a 50 per cent stake in Fitch Group (Reuters 2012). In 2014 Fimalac sold a further 30 per cent of shares to Hearst, for nearly $2 billion, giving Hearst control over Fitch Group with an 80 per cent stake (Fimalac 2014; Alden 2014). On 12 December that year it was announced that the American Hearst Corporation would be the majority owner of Fitch Group. In an effort to preserve the influence of Fimalac's founder and chairman/CEO, Marc Ladreit de Lacharrière, it was announced that he would remain chairman of the Fitch Group's board of directors. As a further part of the deal, Fimalac would retain 50 per cent of the votes on the Fitch Group's board of directors until 2020 (Fimalac 2014). Even though Fimalac's withdrawal was supposed to happen gradually, it came to a rather abrupt end. In 2018 Fimalac sold its 20 per cent minority position to Hearst for $2.8 billion (*Financial Times* 2018a). It had taken Hearst 12 years in total to take full control of Fitch Group, and it spent about $6 billion in total. Questions of desirability aside, it is fair to say that the ambition to establish a truly European CRA in the case of Fitch has failed.

Technological change and the commodification of rating

It goes beyond the scope of this book to discuss the potential implications of what it means that a mass media and business information conglomerate has purchased a CRA, as in the case of Fitch. This development is emblematic of the increasing similarities between the media world and the world of rating, however, which have intensified over recent decades. Legally speaking, as with the work of journalists, ratings are statements of opinion protected by the first amendment to the constitution in the United States, but this is not all. Developments in technology and mass media and the 24-hours news cycle have influenced how the rating industry works in terms of speed and substance. The challenges that rating analysts and journalists face arising from the acceleration of the news cycle are very similar. In journalism, classical "values of verification, proportion, relevance, depth, and quality of interpretation" give way to "sensationalism, entertainment, and opinion". A "journalism of assertion" competes for readers' attention "putting a claim into the arena of public discussion as quickly as possible" (Kovach & Rosenstiel 1999, cited in Weaver *et al.* 2007: 226). The validity of the claim becomes less important than its potential to spark public interest. This is not to say that ratings are at risk of becoming "fake news" in a roundabout way. It would also be too much of a stretch to claim that CRAs will become popular objects of entertainment among students like a Netflix series (even though this would be the best KPI for a scholar such as me).

Speeding up the rating process comes at the cost of rating quality. Pace kills reflective thinking. Ratings increasingly deviate from being well-founded and informed opinions. The acceleration of available information makes it impossible for the rating analyst to do a decent job in spite his or her best efforts. In other words, the 24-hour news cycle undermines the very *raison d'être* of the rating industry, which is to provide sound and reasoned judgement about credit-worthiness. From the investors' perspective, reflection has become redundant in the light of the availability of simple, quick and easily digestible information in the form of ratings. The existence of ratings lulls investors into a false sense of security, facilitating the evasion of reflection. Ironically, the feeling of being overwhelmed increases the investors' cognitive dependence on ratings, while ratings, at the same time, become more ad hoc judgements. In other words, it is a self-reinforcing process.

At least theoretically, the delegation of due diligence would not be a problem under the assumption that rating amounts to sound and reasoned judgement. If the inputs and the processes behind rating are no longer reliable, however, not least because of the 24-hour news cycle, then it becomes problematic. It would certainly be too simplistic to blame it all on the 24-hour news cycle. Nevertheless, it is naïve to overlook the fact that a mass media corporation has become the sole owner of the third largest CRA in the world. We need to be mindful of the structural and technological changes occurring in the media landscape when we analyse the imperatives that the rating industry has been exposed to in recent decades, and how these developments affect the agencies' work and their role in financialized capitalism today and in the future.

Not only has technological change affected how the rating industry works in terms of speed, but it has also influenced the dominant business model. As Krugman (2010) says:

> The rating agencies began as market researchers, selling assessments of corporate debt to people considering whether to buy that debt. Eventually, however, they morphed into something quite different: companies that were hired by the people selling debt to give that debt a seal of approval.

A case in point is the advent of the copying machine, which exacerbated the free-rider problem of the former "investor pays" business model. When an investor mandated and paid a CRA to rate a debt issuer, there was a risk that the rating report would be shared by a multitude of investors. This free-riding risk curtailed the revenue stream of the CRAs. As a result, in the late 1960s and early 1970s the "issuer pays" business model outpaced the "investor pays" business model to become the predominant remuneration model in the rating industry, which it has remained to the present day. CRAs are paid by the issuers of a financial product and not by the investor. In the majority of cases, the CRAs charge fees mostly or exclusively to the issuer.[43]

The "issuer pays" business model gained prominence above all in the wake of the global financial crisis. The over-optimistic ratings of complex, highly structured products, which then turned out to be toxic assets at the peak of the crisis, have been largely related to the conflicts of interest inherent in the "issuer pays" business model. CRAs are incentivized to please debt issuers, who are their customers, more than investors. The distorting effect of the incentive structure on the quality of ratings is a logical consequence of the profit-maximizing rational behaviour of CRAs. The reform efforts after the GFC showed that it is impossible to overcome the "issuer pays" business model. A key reason for this is that the available remuneration alternatives, whether "investor pays", "subscriber pays", user fee or paying for performance compensation, suffer from their own conflicts of interest. As mentioned above, the "investor pays" model is susceptible to free-riding because of the public good aspects inherent in rating (Coffee 2011). As Persaud (2009: 15) puts it succinctly, "In today's information-free, equal-disclosure world, the value of a rating is that everyone knows it. But if everybody already knows it they will not pay for it."

It is fair to say that the GFC has focused the perspective on "issuer pays" and the related conflicts of interest as the main causes of rating failure. Despite the undeniable problematic incentive structures at work in the current business model, we need to open our perspective for more fundamental issues when we problematize rating. One is the commodification of rating itself. Regardless of the business model, the commodification of rating goes hand in hand with a trade-off between profitability, transparency and rating quality. Conflicts of interest are inevitable as long as we stick to the commodification of rating. Moreover, the isolated understanding of credit rating agencies as neutral informational intermediaries whose function is to decrease information asymmetries between borrowers and lenders has led to a neglect of the unintended consequences of the commodification of rating. An appreciation of the actual nature of rating as a public good, given its de facto non-excludability and non-rivalry in consumption, is called for. In turn, this may increase our awareness of the consolidation of private forms of authority that the commodification of rating has produced.

Important though it is to consider the structural conflicts of interest at work in the current commodified rating system, we should beware of reducing all problems of rating to flawed incentives related to the business model. For example, the "issuer pays" business model does not apply for unsolicited ratings, but there are still issues of rating quality, or instances of rating failure. Unsolicited ratings are published without a debt issuer requesting them. Being unsolicited, CRAs rely mainly on publicly available data as the basis for their rating decisions.[44] As a case in point, sovereign governments are usually not customers of CRAs, and most sovereign ratings are issued without a government paying for them, and are thus unsolicited. For example, there is no formal contract between S&P and the German, French or UK government to issue sovereign ratings.[45] The absence of the "issuer pays" business model in the case of unsolicited ratings reverses the logic of conflicts of interest derived from the incentive structure. Consequently, a perspective that emphasizes the role of incentives as motives for individual behaviour infers a less biased sovereign rating. Because the sovereign rating is unsolicited, CRAs would not have an incentive to underestimate risks, favouring the perception of an alleged accuracy of sovereign ratings. Empirical evidence suggests, however, that sovereign ratings, even if unsolicited, can still have serious issues of rating quality, such as being pro-cyclical or inconsistent across countries. This shows that flawed incentive structures related to the commodification of rating cannot fully explain rating failure.

The fact that CRAs do not generate revenue from sovereign ratings as they are unsolicited raises some questions about the motives of CRAs in assessing sovereigns. One rationale for issuing them is the use of sovereign ratings as the benchmark for other issuers of debt (Moody's Investors Service 2012: 3).[46] Another rationale for providing unsolicited sovereign ratings is to offer a complimentary service for investors who want to invest in the sovereign bonds of countries they are not familiar with, and thus need an assessment of creditworthiness. The effort to offer complimentary services to investors shows that, despite the shift in the rating business model from "investor pays" to "issuer pays", the investor still plays a central role as the CRAs' addressee. This investor-centredness is also visible in the names and straplines of the CRAs, such as Moody's *Investors* Service and Fitch's "Know your risk". Therefore, whether the dominant business model in the rating industry is "issuer pays" or "investor pays", the authority of CRAs should not be limited to a zero-sum game between issuers' and investors' interests. There are reasons for rating failure that go beyond an issuer or investor bias. The role of ideas and other non-material factors in influencing rating practices should receive at least as much attention as the conflicts of interest pertinent to the different business models that result from the commodification of rating.

2
WHAT DO CREDIT RATING AGENCIES DO?

The authors of the common language of credit risk

A credit rating agency *rates* the creditworthiness of a bond issuer. But what does this actually mean? Common knowledge in the context of financial markets suggests that rating involves an assessment of creditworthiness, which relies on figures and data conventionally deemed relevant for this purpose. Generally speaking, the verb "to rate" signifies the assignment of "a standard or value to (something) according to a particular scale".[1] In the case of credit rating, the object of the assessment refers to any entity seeking access to capital markets by issuing bonds to satisfy its funding needs, ranging from companies, banks, municipalities and sovereigns to supranationals.[2] In the case of *public* entities, the refinancing through capital markets is not as apolitical as it sounds. When a state or municipality resorts to capital markets, it exposes itself to the CRAs' judgement, becoming subject to the logics and interpretive frameworks of the financial market community. Unlike politically unpopular taxation, a public entity implicitly consents to the rules of the game of the financial market's sphere. Apart from creating a financial dependence, the borrower tacitly accepts that norms, worldviews and ideas preponderant in financial markets transcend and diffuse into the political sphere.

Considering the definition of the verb "to rate" – assigning a standard or value to a particular scale – the specificity of the credit rating scale is that it is created by the CRAs themselves. The same applies to the assigned value – that is, the rating content; scale and value do not exist independently from each other. The scale constitutes the rating content, mirroring how creditworthiness has come to mean "credit rating". Instead of amounting to a quasi-metric that is fungible and transferable to other units of measurement, credit ratings have gained power of definition over creditworthiness: A bond issuer is deemed creditworthy *because* of the top rating, rather than the top rating reflecting a preconceived notion of creditworthiness, which can be transferred to another metric or unit of account. Credit ratings create predictability by themselves.

How have ratings come to mean, and, therefore, be constitutive of, credit-worthiness? In his autobiography, John Moody summed up the investors' dilemma at the time when he founded the company: "A high percentage of corporation securities had to be bought on faith rather than knowledge" (Moody 1933: 90, cited in Sinclair 2005: 23). If, almost a century later, credit ratings constitute creditworthiness, then, in John Moody's words, knowledge has, to a certain degree, become faith again. Two related aspects have been crucial in this regard, reflecting a certain irony of history: the very success factor of rating, namely their representation in alphanumerical letter grades; and the consequence of the agencies' success – that is, their authoritative standing.

Through their "distinctively portable format and scientific appearance" (Carruthers 2013: 544), credit ratings function as a universal, easy-to-understand language of credit risk. Credit ratings provide a "simplified vocabulary and conceptual framework through which to talk about credit risk" (Bruner & Abdelal 2005: 206). It lies in the nature of a language to develop a life of its own. It can be used with ease by others than just its authors. But it also sets the precondition that the rating symbol becomes constitutive of creditworthiness, and thus an object of faith, as market participants rely on it without substantially questioning what knowledge is processed inside – a typical feature of a language (imagine questioning everything as you are talking). This conflicts sharply with what John Moody had in mind when he turned the business idea of rating into reality.

As it is the value proposition of rating to go beyond pure description by making judgements about debtors' creditworthiness in the form of letter grades, the CRAs' rhetorical insistence on paraphrasing the rating content as "qualitative (nominal) information" or "opinion" is historically misleading. The CRAs' legal status as first amendment "opinion-expressing" entities, which serves as a protective legal shield against accountability (Bruner & Abdelal 2005: 210), does not help to clarify the matter. If CRAs admitted and stood by the fact that they are issuing judgements, this would not only do justice to their success story but would likewise reveal their epistemic authority. Their unwillingness (at least in the past) to do exactly this suggests that CRAs have an ambivalent relationship with their authoritative status. For example, in the aftermath of the financial crisis CRAs in part welcomed the idea of reducing the reliance on CRA ratings in regulatory frameworks such as Basel III, which can be interpreted as a confession and a shying away from their accumulated power (Hinrichs 2012; Mennillo & Roy 2014).[3] As CRAs come to realize that denying their authority puts them in an unfavourable light, it is not surprising that in the meantime S&P Global Ratings is vocal in openly claiming "unparalleled thought leadership".[4]

The rating scale

Table 2.1 displays the rating scales of the Big Three. Usually, sovereigns, corporates and insurance companies are rated according to this scale, which is termed the "long-term rating scale", to be precise.[5]

Although the alphanumerical signs come in different variations and combinations, the usage of letter grades automatically triggers the association with school grades predominantly used in the Anglo-Saxon education system (*Guardian* 2009): "These companies act like teachers, grading every nation according to the state of their economy, their public finances and the risk of things going wrong in the future. The lower the credit rating, the higher the cost of borrowing." In fact, during the euro crisis in the wake of the GFC, "doing one's homework" (*Guardian* 2012; EUobserver 2012) has been used as a metaphor for the countries' need to undertake prescribed reforms in order to restore their sovereign creditworthiness and, thereby, to upgrade the rating.

In the following, I will examine the essential characteristics of the rating scale. First, the rating scale is ordinal. This means it ranks the creditworthiness

Table 2.1 Long-term rating scales of issuer credit ratings

S&P	Fitch	Moody's
AAA	AAA	Aaa
AA+	AA+	Aa1
AA	AA	Aa2
AA–	AA–	Aa3
A+	A+	A1
A	A	A2
A–	A–	A3
BBB+	BBB+	Baa1
BBB	BBB	Baa2
BBB–	BBB–	Baa3
BB+	BB+	Ba1
BB	BB	Ba2
BB–	BB–	Ba3
B+	B+	B1
B	B	B2
B–	B–	B3
CCC+	CCC+	Caa1
CCC	CCC	Caa2
CCC–	CCC–	Caa3
CC	CC	Ca
C	C	C
SD/D	RD/D	

Sources: Fitch Ratings (2020: 21), Standard & Poor's (2014: 7) and Moody's Investors Service (2020a: 6).

of issuers according to an order, with "A" ratings at the top, "B" ratings as the second-best category, and so on. Keeping this in mind is particularly important, as it cautions us against mistaking ratings for the probability of defaults. Fitch states that the "ordinal ranking of issuers [is] based on the agency's view of their relative vulnerability to default, rather than a prediction of a specific percentage likelihood of default" (Fitch Ratings 2013a: 9). Second, the rating scale is relative, meaning that the grades are not to be understood in an absolute sense but in a relative sense.

If ratings are, by definition, relative assessments of creditworthiness, then this implies that there always has to be a role model, a benchmark within a given class of debt issuers. For example, in the case of sovereign ratings, by necessity there is a sovereign that constitutes "best practice". A prominent example is Germany within the eurozone. "German bunds" – i.e. bonds issued by the German government – are seen as "safe haven" assets because of the hitherto unquestioned creditworthiness of its issuer. When other euro-using countries came under financial distress in the course of the financial crisis of 2008, they faced rating downgrades. In order to increase their competitiveness, the CRAs (among others) promoted internal deflation, also known as austerity, and Germany's export-oriented growth model served as a role model.[6]

In times of a systemic shock that affects all sovereigns – whether an exogenous one, as in the Covid-19 crisis, or an endogenous one, as with the 2008 GFC – "best practice" needs to be redefined. With a benchmark lacking, it becomes tricky for CRAs to diagnose a policy error (or the absence of it). It is in these moments that the relative rating scale is challenged. This is when CRAs redefine market orthodoxy, manifesting their epistemic authority. In normal times CRAs reproduce market orthodoxy. But, even in this case, the relative rating scale can put the CRAs under pressure when there are deviations between the United States, the benchmark "triple A" country par excellence, and the current orthodox mindset. A reproach of "home bias" may be raised against the CRAs (Fuchs & Gehring 2017). Another illustration of the intricacies of the relative rating scale is S&P's downgrade of the United States in 2011 (Reuters 2011b; CNN Money 2011). The market reactions to the downgrade were remarkable: Treasury bills (T-bills) rose in value, and yields went down. Market reactions to downgrades of other sovereigns usually move in the other direction. Paradoxically, it was the uncertainty that the US downgrade created that led to a run into T-bills, as these are treated globally as "safe haven" assets. The market reaction also demonstrated an unshakable belief in the dollar and US creditworthiness. Instead of being a home bias, the United States' top rating may actually be no more than the CRAs' reproduction of this market belief – or, returning to the relativity of the rating scale, the market reaction to the US downgrade could be read as the market's anticipation of the impossibility of not having a benchmark country.

Both Moody's and S&P have nine major rating categories each; Fitch has ten. These categories can be additionally differentiated through the usage of modifiers. Fitch Ratings (2013a: 10) states that the "modifiers '+' or '–' may be appended to a rating to denote relative status within" those major categories. Likewise, Standard & Poor's (2012b: 7) notes that ratings "may be modified by the addition of a plus (+) or minus (–) sign to show relative standing within the major rating categories". Both CRAs emphasize the latent character of the usage of modifiers, which allows the possibility of a more fine-tuned differentiation of the rating scale, apart from "outlook" changes and further differentiation tools, such as putting debt issuers "on watch" or publishing announcements and comments.

Moody's uses an alternative rating scale, which combines the capital letters (A, B, C) with the lowercase letter "a" to form the major rating categories. It also uses numerical modifiers (1, 2, 3) instead of (+, –), deviating from the Anglo-Saxon grading style (Moody's Investors Service 2013b: 5): "1 indicates that the obligation ranks in the higher end of its generic rating category; the modifier 2 indicates a mid-range ranking; and the modifier 3 indicates a ranking in the lower end of that generic rating category." The numerical format leads to a compelling, visible assignment of modifiers. By contrast, in the case of S&P and Fitch, the usage of (+, –) is optional, so therefore mid-range ratings within major categories lack modifiers. Despite these differences, in all three cases the application of modifiers excludes the top end of the rating scale: for Moody's, modifiers range from rating category "Aa" to "Caa"; for S&P, from "AA" to "CCC"; and, for Fitch, from "AA" to "B". With Moody's and S&P, the low end of the rating scale stops using modifiers one rating category before default (or selective default). Fitch, on the other hand, stops assigning modifiers three categories before default (or restricted default). Another commonality of the rating scales of the Big Three refers to the subtle logic of quantification inherent in the apposition of the latter grades: the tripling and doubling of the letters points to a logic of "the more letters, the better the rating", in each major rating category. For Moody's, the higher the quantity of the lower-case letter "a" appended to the original letter grade, the better the rating. Further differentiation by the numerical modifiers, with "1" ranking the best in the concerned rating category, reproduces the ordinal character of the overall rating scale.

Investment grade, or not investment grade; that is the question

Taking a step back, let us look at the big picture of the long-term rating scale. Table 2.1 is divided by a horizontal line in the middle of the rating categories, which depicts the investment grade threshold. Ratings above the line comprise the investment grade category; ratings below the line belong to the speculative grade category. The latter is often informally referred to as "junk" by market participants and the general public, including the media. Of course, such terminology does not belong to the CRAs' official PR repertoire, even though a high-ranked CRA representative involuntarily may use it in public (as during an academic panel discussion in late 2012, for which he apologized).

According to the capacity to meet financial commitments, investment-grade issuers are rated along the continuum starting from "extremely strong" to "very strong" to "strong" to "adequate".[7] Regarding the speculative grade, Standard & Poor's (2012b: 7) maintains that, although obligors "will likely have some quality and protective characteristics, these may be outweighed by large uncertainties or major exposures to adverse conditions". The more vulnerable obligors are, the more dependent they are on favourable "business, financial and economic conditions to meet financial commitments" (*ibid.*: 7), which means a lower speculative grade.[8] Tables 2.2 and 2.3 summarize the meaning of the mid-range ratings per major rating category, for investment-grade ratings and for speculative-grade ratings, respectively.[9]

The halving of the rating scale is commonly considered as a market convention that "established ... over time as shorthand to describe the categories 'AAA' to 'BBB' (investment grade) and 'BB' to 'D' (speculative grade)" (Fitch Ratings 2013a: 6). Accordingly, there is no official distinction between investment grade and speculative grade. To limit the division of the rating scale into investment and speculative grade to a market habit is, to say the least, a bit of an understatement. It matters far beyond that. It is of enormous institutional relevance and has great implications for capital allocation. Whether a bond is rated investment grade or not is decisive for it to make it on the books of a pension fund, for example. The question of investment or speculative grade has found its way not only into the investment standards of institutional investors but also into the investment guidelines of public monetary authorities.

Table 2.2 Meaning of investment-grade rating categories

Rating	Meaning
AAA/Aaa	Highest credit quality; lowest expectation of default risk; exceptionally strong capacity to meet financial commitment; highly unlikely to be adversely affected by foreseeable events.
AA/Aa2	Very high credit quality; expectations of very low default/credit risk; very strong capacity for payment of financial commitments; capacity not significantly vulnerable to foreseeable events; differs from above only to a small degree.
A/A2	High credit quality; expectations of low default/credit risk; capacity for payment of financial commitments still strong; capacity may nevertheless be more vulnerable to adverse business or economic conditions than above.
BBB/Baa2	Good credit quality; expectations of default risk currently low; capacity for payment of financial commitments adequate, but adverse business or economic conditions more likely to impair capacity to meet financial commitment; moderate credit risk; speculative characteristics.

Table 2.3 Meaning of non-investment-grade/speculative rating categories

Rating	Meaning
BB/Ba2	Speculative; elevated vulnerability to default risk, particularly in the event of adverse changes in business or economic conditions; business or financial flexibility exists, however, which supports the servicing of financial commitments; less vulnerable in the near term than below, but ongoing uncertainties and exposure to adverse business, financial or economic conditions, which could lead to inadequate capacity to meet financial commitments
B/B2	Highly speculative; material default risk present, but a limited margin of safety remains; financial commitments are currently being met, but capacity for continued payment is vulnerable to deterioration in the business and economic environment; adverse business, financial, or economic conditions will probably impair the capacity or willingness to meet financial commitments
CCC/Caa2	Substantial credit risk; default a real possibility; vulnerable; dependent upon favourable business, financial and economic conditions to meet financial commitments.
CC/Ca	Currently highly vulnerable; highly speculative; probably in, or very near, default, with some prospect of recovery of principal and interest.
C	Bankruptcy petition filed or similar action taken; payments of financial commitments continued.
SD/RD/D	Selective default/restricted default/payment default on financial commitments.

For example, bonds and other marketable assets have to be investment grade in order to qualify for the European Central Bank's (ECB's) expanded asset purchasing programme or in order to be accepted as collateral (ECB 2015). The Eurosystem credit assessment framework (ECAF) for the monetary policy operations of the ECB is defined according to the Eurosystem's harmonized rating scale. The minimum standard of "credit quality step 3" of the harmonized rating scale plays a crucial role in the central bank's collateral eligibility standards and other ECB operations, such as the above-mentioned expanded asset purchasing programme of 2015. On closer examination, the lower bound of credit quality step 3 refers to the CRAs' investment-grade thresholds: in Fitch and S&P terms, a minimum long-term rating of BBB−; and, in Moody's terms, Baa3.[10] That the low end of the ECB's credit quality steps corresponds to the threshold between the investment and non-investment grade categories of the CRAs emphasizes not only the central banks' orientation towards the epistemic authority of CRAs in terms of credit-worthiness assessment, but also that the distinction between investment grade and non-investment grade is much more than an informal market convention.

The question of investment grade or not also plays a fundamental role in the context of the Covid-19 pandemic. CRAs indirectly influence which corporations have access to capital in financial distress and under what conditions. At the end of March 2020 the Federal Reserve in the United States took unprecedented steps to mitigate the impact of the crisis on global financial markets and the US economy. Among others, it announced that it would buy investment-grade corporate bonds (Bloomberg 2020). Examples of these Fed programmes that support investment-grade corporate debt are the Primary Dealer Credit Facility (PDCF), the Primary Market Corporate Credit Facility (PMCCF) and the Secondary Market Corporate Credit Facility (SMCCF). For the latter two programmes, the Fed has not limited their size, and the Treasury backstops each with $10 billion, as of this writing. In order to be eligible for these emergency facilities, a US corporation that issues corporate debt in the primary market needs to be rated as investment grade. Those corporate bonds that are already circulating in the secondary market need to be investment grade in order to be bought by the Fed. And, likewise, only ETFs that invest in investment-grade debt can qualify for these programmes.

In turn, when a bond is at risk of losing its investment-grade status, it also loses its eligibility as an asset for institutional investors and for financing facilities in times of crisis. The debt issuer faces a fire sale, which will be even more detrimental for its financial condition, as it depresses the price of the bond and increases its risk premium. This means that the borrower needs to pay higher interest rates to investors. With this in mind, it is surely no exaggeration to conclude that rating actions are fateful for debt issuers especially at the lower margin of the upper half of the rating scale. The halving of the rating scale matters far more than the idea of a casual market convention would lead you believe.

Rating methodologies

CRAs employ different rating methodologies according to issuer type. For illustrative purposes in this book, I focus on sovereign, sub-sovereign and corporate ratings. This will offer a general sense of how CRAs work. Before we go into the specificities of the different methodologies, the flow chart in Figure 2.1 illustrates the general steps of the rating process.[11]

Sovereigns

In order to understand why certain political, economic or social occurrences affect a country's sovereign rating, it is important to know what a sovereign rating is, and what the assessment consists of. Sovereign ratings deliver qualitative information about a "sovereign government's willingness and ability to service its debt on time and in full" (Standard & Poor's 2012a: 3). The gauging of a government's willingness to pay or not to pay is a unique characteristic of the sovereign creditworthiness assessment. Fitch Ratings (2012: 1) defines a sovereign issuer default rating (IDR) as "a forward-looking assessment of a sovereign's

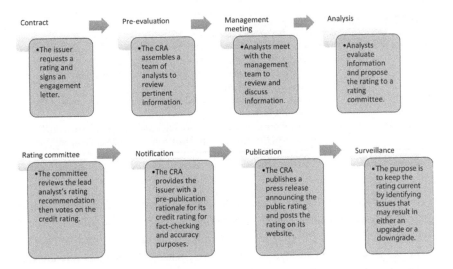

Figure 2.1 Steps of the rating process
Note: ICR = issuer credit rating

capacity and willingness to honour its existing and future obligations in full and on time". Moody's Investors Service (2013b: 4) defines sovereign ratings as "forward-looking opinions of the relative credit risks of financial obligations" issued by the respective sovereigns. Moody's Investors Service (2002: 3) notes the importance of the forward-looking character of the sovereign analysis when evaluating the risk of default over a medium- to long-term time horizon. Merely using backward-looking quantitative data of the "historical performance of the economy" would not be enough: "[E]xamination of past experience has to be supplemented by ... the construction of a range of scenarios that stress-test the vulnerability of a country's economic, political and financial situation" (*ibid.*: 3).

Therefore, a sovereign rating is not a quantitative measurement of sovereign default risk but a nominal opinion of an anticipated future in a quasi-quantitative guise. Moody's also emphasizes the distinct role of national governments in their capacity of sovereign bond issuers as the largest borrowers of the "vast majority of the world's debt capital markets" (Moody's Investors Service 2012: 3):

> A number of characteristics distinguish sovereign bond issuers from other debtors and inform the approach to assessing creditworthiness. These characteristics include (i) a sovereign's ability to modify the taxation of its citizenship in order to generate revenue with which to service outstanding debt; (ii) freedom from a higher authority to compel debt resolution and relieve the obligation of collateral; and (iii) the high probability of survival even after an event of default (i.e. countries rarely disappear).

Table 2.4 Key sovereign rating inputs

Standard & Poor's	Political risk; economic structure; economic growth prospects; fiscal flexibility; general government debt burden; offshore and contingent liabilities; monetary flexibility; external liquidity; external debt burden.
Moody's	Economic strength; institutional strength; financial strength of the government; susceptibility to event risk.
Fitch	Macroeconomic policies, performance and prospects; structural features of the economy; public finances; external finances.

Source: IMF (2010: 99).

S&P also emphasizes the special role of governments as debt issuers, since "creditors have only limited legal redress" (Standard & Poor's 2017b: 9). A government may be able to repay its debt and have the capacity, but be unwilling to do so. This suggests an asymmetrical power relation between sovereigns and investors in favour of the former. Empirical evidence suggests otherwise, however (see, for example, Roos 2019).

Table 2.4 gives an overview of the main inputs the Big Three use for their sovereign ratings. According to the sovereign rating methodology published by S&P in 2017 (Standard & Poor's 2017b: 3), "[b]oth quantitative factors and qualitative considerations" form the basis for the following five "forward-looking assessments":[12]

- institutional:[13] institutional effectiveness and political risks
- economic: economic structure and growth prospects
- external: external liquidity and international investment position
- fiscal: fiscal performance and flexibility, debt burden
- monetary: monetary flexibility

Further, the methodology states that "[e]ach of the above mentioned five factors is assessed on a six-point numerical scale from '1' (strongest) to '6' (weakest)" (*ibid.*). The "average" of the institutional assessment and the economic assessment constitutes the "sovereign's institutional and economic profile" (*ibid.*). The average of the external assessment, the fiscal assessment and the monetary assessment makes up the "flexibility and performance profile". These two profiles determine the "indicative rating level", as shown in Figure 2.2. The indicative rating level is then used as a basis for discussion at the committee meeting preceding the rating decision.

Assessing on a numerical scale (i.e. de facto assigning scores), calculating averages and combining them in an additive fashion suggest the transparency and traceability of the sovereign rating methodology. Many of the inputs actually evade quantification, however, and are a judgement call. This shows how, right at

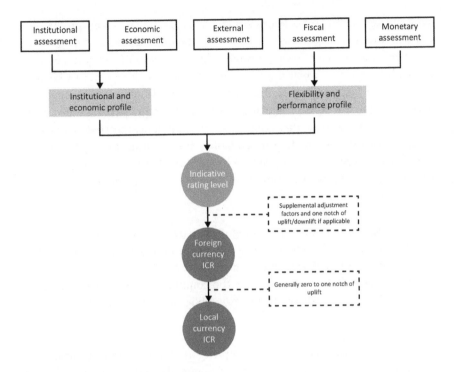

Figure 2.2 Sovereign rating criteria, S&P
Source: Standard & Poor's (2017b: 2).

the early stages of the rating construction, the mimicking of calculation is already occurring. To a certain extent, the indicative rating level already conceals the contentiousness of the inputs it consists of.

In order to get a sense of the meaning of the scores, let us consider the definition of "institutional assessment" (*ibid.*):

> The institutional assessment reflects our view of how a government's institutions and policymaking affect a sovereign's credit fundamentals by delivering sustainable public finances, promoting balanced economic growth, and responding to economic or political shocks. It also reflects our view of the transparency and accountability of data, processes, and institutions; a sovereign's debt repayment culture; and potential external and domestic security risks.

Finally, the committee meetings are the last stage of a sovereign rating decision. The "final rating assigned by the committee is primarily determined by applying the rating criteria to the information that the analysts have collected and evaluated" (Standard & Poor's 2012a: 6).[14] According to a high-profile CRA representative in charge of sovereign ratings, the rating decision is the product of a "democratic process".[15] The committee board consists of an uneven number of members, so that, when they vote, it is a majority decision. This board is composed of international analysts and senior staff (American, French and German in the case of S&P), which suggests that the agency is concerned about impartiality. Rating criteria are discussed critically in those meetings. Ultimately, drawing on the definition of sovereign ratings, the assessment of a government's "willingness" to repay its debt cannot be quantified and, necessarily, requires deliberation. In terms of the committee meetings, Standard & Poor's (2012a: 7) stresses the following:

> However, rather than providing a strictly formulaic assessment, Standard & Poor's factors into its ratings the perceptions and insights of its analysts based on their consideration of all of the information they have obtained. This process helps the committee to form its opinion of an issuer's overall ability to repay obligations in accordance with their terms.

The committee discussion gives the impression of a well-thought-out process behind the sovereign rating decision. Consequently, and some may say paradoxically, awareness of this component of the methodology tends to enhance the credibility of the rating, instead of casting more doubt on it. Reportedly, these discussions involve "intangible issues such as a government's propensity for 'orthodox' vs 'heterodox' policy responses when under acute debt-service" (Bruner & Abdelal 2005: 198).

Precisely because the committee discussion is decisive in the sovereign rating process (even more so in times of crises), it is hardly possible to retrace rating decisions by means of an econometric algorithm. The deliberative element is a consequence of the lack of a strict formulaic methodology and testifies to the essence of rating being a judgement.

The sovereign rating methodology of Moody's is summarized in Figure 2.3. The assessment of "sovereign credit risk" is based on four key factors: economic strength, institutional strength, fiscal strength and susceptibility to event risk. Economic strength is divided into sub-factors, such as growth dynamics, the scale of the economy and national income. Institutional strength is subdivided into "institutional framework and effectiveness" and "policy credibility and effectiveness". The former is measured with indicators such as the Worldwide Government Effectiveness Index, Worldwide Rule of Law Index and the Worldwide Control of Corruption Index. The latter captures inflation data. Fiscal strength comprises data about the ratios of government debt to GDP

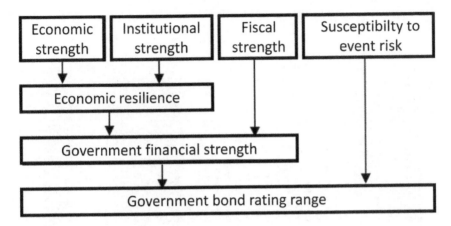

Figure 2.3 Sovereign rating criteria, Moody's
Source: Moody's Investors Service (2018a: 4).

and government interest payments to GDP, among others. The last factor, susceptibility to event risk, includes sub-factors such as political risk, government liquidity risk, banking sector risk and external vulnerability risk.

Similarly, Fitch's sovereign rating analysis is based on four analytical pillars (Fitch Ratings 2018: 1).

1. Structural features of the economy that render it more or less vulnerable to shocks, including the risks posed by the financial sector, political risk and governance factors.
2. Macroeconomic performance, policies and prospects, including growth prospects, economic stability and the coherence and credibility of policy.
3. Public finances, including budget balances, the structure and sustainability of public debt and fiscal financing and the likelihood of the crystallization of contingent liabilities.
4. External finances, including the sustainability of current account balances and capital flows, and the level and structure of external debt (public and private).

Figure 2.4 summarizes the rating criteria of Fitch Ratings. Regarding the weightings, Fitch states that "structural features typically carry the highest weight within the analysis" (*ibid*.). The published methodology remains vague about the weights of the other three pillars: even though they are "typically lower", in crisis situations "this can vary" (*ibid*.).

As can be derived from Figure 2.4, the sovereign rating is the product of an interplay between the "sovereign rating model" and qualitative considerations captured as "qualitative overlay", which can lead to "notching adjustments" – that

	Analytical pillar	Structural features	Macroeconomic performance, policies and prospects	Public finances	External finances	Output/notching adjustment
Input	Key criteria factors	• Governance quality • Wealth and flexibility of economy • Political stability and capacity • Financial sector risks	• Policy framework • GDP growth • Inflation • Real effective exchange rate	• Government debt • Fiscal balance • Debt dynamics • Fiscal policy	• Balance of payments • External balance sheet • External liquidity	Long-term foreign currency IDR equivalent
Sovereign Rating Model (SRM)	Regression-based, point-in-time Rating model based on 18 key variables designed to replicate Fitch's Sovereign Rating Criteria	• Governance indicators • GDP per capita • Share in world GDP • Years since default or restructuring event • Broad money supply	• Real GDP growth volatility • Consumer price inflation • Real GDP growth	• Gross government debt/GDP • General government interest (% of revs) • General government fiscal balance/GDP • Foreign currency government debt/general government debt	• Reserve currency flexibility • Sovereign net foreign assets (% of GDP) • Commodity dependence • Foreign exchange reserves (months of current external payments) • External interest service (% of current external receipts) • Current account balance + foreign direct investment (% of GDP)	
Qualitative Overlay (QO)	Forward-looking adjustment framework to provide a subjective assessment of key criteria factors that are not explicitly included in the SRM	• Political stability • Banking sector and macroprudential risks • Business environment and economic flexibility	• Macroeconomic policy framework • GDP growth outlook (5 years) • Macroeconomic stability	• Fiscal financing flexibility • Public debt sustainability • Fiscal structure	• External financing flexibility • External debt sustainability • Vulnerability to shocks	
Potential QO notching adjustment		+2 to −2	+2 to −2	+2 to −2	+2 to −2	+3 to −3*
Final rating outcome						Final long-term foreign currency IDR

*Except in certain circumstances when, at the judgement of the committee, notching can be extended.

Figure 2.4 Sovereign rating criteria, Fitch Ratings
Source: Fitch Ratings (2018: 2).

is to say, variations of the rating grade from the pure model outcome. Apart from exceptional circumstances, the adjustment is limited within a specific range of + 3/–3 notches for each rating, and +2/–2 per analytical pillar. In the end, it is the committee that has the final say with its judgement.

Consequently, the extent to which political occurrences affect the institutional assessment and, therefore, have an impact (or not) on the rating can be a matter of controversy. Take, for example, the "inconclusive" election results in Italy in early 2013. These induced Fitch to downgrade Italy to BBB+ with a negative outlook on 8 March 2013 (Fitch Ratings 2013b). For S&P, however, the election results were not a rationale to take immediate rating action: S&P downgraded Italy only to BBB from BBB+ four months later, in July 2013, because of a lack of reform (BBC News 2013). For Moody's, the election gave rise only indirectly to an affirmation of Italy's Baa2 government rating and negative outlook on 26 April 2013: "Italy's economic outlook remains weak due to a number of factors. Firstly, low consumer and investor confidence, in part reflecting the inconclusive election outcome and uncertain political prospects, together with rising unemployment, are weakening domestic demand" (Moody's Investors Service 2013c). Each CRA's view legitimizes rating action or inaction. It is almost impossible to detect a methodology-deviating pattern. To a certain extent, the sovereign rating methodology is self-immunizing with respect to criticism, given the implicit room for manoeuvre.

BOX 2: SOVEREIGN RATING SPECIFICITIES

Foreign and local currency

CRAs distinguish between sovereign ratings in foreign and local currency. The difference lies in the obligor's capacity to meet its obligations denominated in either the local or foreign currency. In the case of S&P, for example, the sovereign local currency rating is usually not more than one notch higher than the foreign currency rating. The reason why the sovereign local currency rating is higher than the foreign one arises from the fact that the sovereign's creditworthiness in local currency can be supported by currency manipulation powers; a sovereign has the authority to issue local currency through its central bank. Moreover, the regulatory control over its own domestic financial system is also conducive to the local currency's creditworthiness. Only if a sovereign is a member of a monetary union – as in the case of the eurozone – or when it uses a currency of another sovereign, then the local currency rating will be the same as the foreign currency rating (such as the principality of Liechtenstein, as it uses the Swiss franc as legal tender). In the case of Moody's, the differentiation between local and foreign currency ratings is to recognize the problems of servicing debts in one currency spilling over and affecting a government's ability to service its debt in another. There can be rating gaps between a government's local and foreign currency bond ratings when there is limited capital mobility or when the government is facing constraint in external liquidity or showing a distinction in its ability to repay debt in local and foreign currency.

Short-term and long-term

There is also a distinction between short-term and long-term issuer credit ratings that applies to sovereigns. Considering the maturity of sovereign bonds, the long-term rating is usually deemed relevant for sovereigns as issuers. Sovereigns may sometimes also issue commercial papers with shorter duration, however, for which a short-term rating is needed (Standard & Poor's 2017b: 32).

The national credit rating scale

There is also a further differentiation between the classical sovereign rating scale and the national credit rating scale. National scale ratings are opinions of creditworthiness relative to issuers and issues *within* a single country's jurisdiction or monetary union. For Fitch, they are used in emerging markets with low investment-grade sovereign ratings. The national scale enables greater rating differentiation within a market than the international scale (with which sovereign ratings are determined), especially in highly speculative-grade countries, for which ratings tend to cluster around low sovereign ratings.

Sub-sovereigns

In the following, I look at the way CRAs assess sub-sovereign issuers. Depending on the definitions provided by each CRA, sub-sovereign entities include municipalities and provincial and regional governmental entities. To get a sense of rated issuers in this category, a few examples: Aberdeen City Council (Scotland, United Kingdom); region of Abruzzo (Italy); municipality of Alba Iulia (Romania); city of Athens (Greece); and Autonomous Region of Azores (Portugal).

As an illustrative case, let us consider the methodology of Moody's in rating sub-sovereigns. It should be noted that, for Moody's, sub-sovereigns are entities outside the United States and include municipalities, provincial and regional governmental entities, but exclude municipal enterprises. As with sovereigns, sub-sovereigns are considered public issuers, because they are generally responsible for the delivery of public services and infrastructural development supported by taxation, fees or transfers from other governments or entities.

Moody's approach to rate sub-sovereigns, or "regional and local governments (RLGs)", as it calls them, is based upon two pillars: "the baseline credit", which is the government's stand-alone intrinsic strength; and "extraordinary support", which refers to support in instances of liquidity stress (Moody's Investors Service 2018b).

The "baseline credit" assessment includes the regular support rendered by domestic governments to their sub-sovereign entities, such as ongoing annual subsidies. Figure 2.5 summarizes how the baseline credit assessment comes about. The consideration of idiosyncratic risk and systemic risk is crucial. As in the case of sovereign ratings, the use of a matrix and the assigning of scores determines the indicative rating level. In the end, however, it is still a judgement.

"Extraordinary support" refers to the likelihood of a "higher-tier government … provid[ing] financial support or other contractual protections to [an RLG] undergoing acute liquidity stress, or to avoid a default on the RLG's debt obligations" (*ibid*.: 25). Manifestations of support can range from one-off cash transfers or other means of external financing. Moody's considers three aspects to extraordinary support: first, the rating of the supporting government; second, the estimated default correlation between the two entities; third, the estimated likelihood of extraordinary government support.

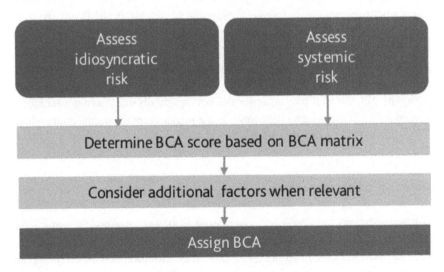

Figure 2.5 Moody's baseline credit assessment (BCA) for sub-sovereigns
Source: Moody's Investors Service (2018b: 4).

To conclude, there are a few important observations to make regarding the politics in all this. First, in the case of sub-sovereigns, both access to liquidity and the level of dependence between the regional and the sovereign are strong determinants of credit risk compared to other factors such as the macroeconomic environment, which is usually one of the most important factors for sovereign rating assessments. Since sub-sovereigns are heavily reliant on their sovereigns, any downgrade of the national government has negative consequences for the sub-sovereign level as well. Second, the financial flexibility "to change the level and nature of spending" (*ibid*.: 9) into the provision of public goods is deemed as something positive for the overall rating of the sub-sovereign. This "fiscal flexibility" implies that the regional government exerts effective control over its operating expenditures. The higher the share it can control, the higher the flexibility, and the better the creditworthiness assessment. Provided that cuts to public services or the change of service standards are "politically acceptable at the local level" (*ibid*.), this includes the option of privatizations. The CRA's methodology remains silent on the definition of what is exactly meant by "politically acceptable", however. Furthermore, the provision of public goods by a public entity needs to be "financially sustainable" and "self-supporting" (*ibid*.: 11). Otherwise, in the event that there are direct subsidies to support the entity in question, this will add to the sub-sovereign's debt profile (*ibid*.): "Our assessment of the self-supporting nature of a government-owned entity is typically based on whether it is financially sustainable in the absence of any ongoing direct subsidy from the RLG."

What looks like a neutral and indisputable statement at first sight is revealed to be highly political on closer inspection. If we take a step back, why should a government-owned entity follow commercial principles at all? Is not the very nature of an entity that provides public goods defined by the fact that its purpose escapes financial accounting rules? In this sense, the success of a public health or education system cannot be measured by the financial revenue it generates. Such an entity cannot be run with the same goal and logics as a profit-driven company. Yet, if it is, it may compromise why it actually exists as a government-owned entity. It may lose its legitimacy in the provision of the public good, which could turn out to be self-defeating.

Corporate rating methodology

Corporate ratings are commonly considered to be the core business of CRAs. When rating analysts rate corporate issuers, they first generate business and financial risk profiles of the companies they assess. These two profiles are then combined to form an "issuer's anchor" (Standard & Poor's 2013b: 2, para. 11). In the second step, six modifiers are analysed that may impact the CRA's anchor conclusion by one or more notches each. These modifiers take into account information about business diversification, capital structure, financial policy, liquidity and management, among others. The outcome of this assessment results in a "stand-alone credit profile" (*ibid.*: 1, para. 1). This profile normally constitutes the corporate credit rating, unless there is "ongoing support" or "negative influence" from a group or government (for government-related entities), which may affect the final issuer credit rating. Figure 2.6 summarizes the corporate rating methodology by S&P.

The financial risk profile consists of an assessment of cash flow and leverage. For this profile, mostly quantitative measures are used (*ibid.*: 3, para. 16). The business risk profile is constituted by three analytic factors: country risk, industry risk and competitive position. Each risk dimension is assigned a numerical value on a scale from 1 to 6 (1 being a very low risk, or excellent competitive position, respectively). It would be erroneous to assume that the different analytic ingredients consist only of quantitative information. As with the assessment of sovereigns, the business risk profile of a company is a "blend of qualitative assessments and quantitative information" (*ibid.*: 3, para. 15). The evaluation of a company's "capacity to generate cash flows in order to service its obligations in a timely fashion" (*ibid.*: 4, para. 20) also escapes exclusive quantification and reminds us that, in the end, corporate ratings too are judgements and not metrics.

A "country risk" is defined (Standard & Poor's 2013a: 1, para. 2) "as the broad range of economic, institutional, financial market, and legal risks that arise from doing business with or in a specific country and can affect a non-sovereign entity's credit quality". For example, legal risks refer to the payment culture or the status of the rule of law in a country to which a corporate issuer has some of its operations or assets exposed. These type of risks are country-specific,

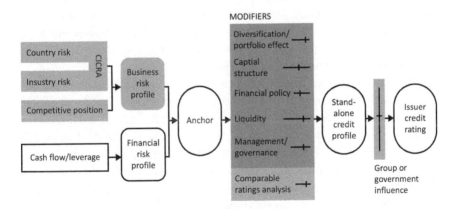

Figure 2.6 Corporate rating methodology, S&P
Source: Standard & Poor's (2013b: 3).

and they indirectly predetermine the highest credit rating achievable for a debt issuer whose transactions are generated in a particular country (this is why it is sometimes also referred to as the "country ceiling", for example, by Moody's). In the case of S&P, there is an explicit differentiation between country risk and sovereign rating. Relevant country risks for corporate issuers would be different from the "likelihood that a sovereign obligor will pay its debt on time and in full" (*ibid.*: 2, para. 11); sovereign ratings capture the credit risk associated with government-issued debt in particular. Sovereign rating analysis "may understate or overstate" (*ibid.*) country-specific risks that are relevant for corporate ratings.

Despite these nuanced differences, through the concept of country risk or sovereign ceilings, the ratings of corporations (and other issuers such as financial institutions) are tied to the perception of their government's creditworthiness. This link between sovereigns and corporations has important implications. First, domestic firms, driven by self-interest to preserve their refinancing ability on capital markets, are inclined to pressurize their governments if the sovereign rating is at risk of deteriorating. For example, the resignation of former Italian prime minister Silvio Berlusconi at the end of 2011 is a pertinent example of the political consequences of rating-induced market pressure on a domestic government (*New York Times* 2011).

Second, to mitigate the dependence on their own sovereign, institutions have an incentive to diversify their sovereign bond portfolio, thus contributing to the international mobility of sovereign debt and rendering the concept of investor loyalty irrelevant (Gabor & Ban 2014). Third, sovereign ceilings exacerbate the impact of sovereign rating downgrades on national economies in bad times. Empirical research has shown that national stock market indexes have a downward trend if their sovereigns are downgraded, which can be linked to the country risk ceiling (see, for example, Brooks *et al.* 2004). As we can see, the concept of sovereign ceiling contributes to the pro-cyclical nature of sovereign ratings, a self-reinforcing dynamic of sovereign rating downgrades that can bring national economies close to a cliff edge in bad times.

Let us return to the general discussion of the corporate rating methodology. Apart from the country risk, another element of the business risk profile is industry risk. Industry risk captures "the relative health and stability of the markets in which a company operates" (Standard & Poor's 2013b: 4, para. 21). Among other things, it contains quantitative information such as the "historical cyclicality of revenues and profits" (*ibid.*: 3, para. 15). The third input for the business risk profile is the assessment of a company's competitive position. The best-positioned companies are considered to be those that have a "competitive advantage and a stronger business risk profile", meaning that they are able "to take advantage of key industry drivers or to mitigate associated risks more effectively" (*ibid.*: 4, para. 23). In contrast, those companies considered less competitive "lack a strong value proposition or are more vulnerable to industry risks" (*ibid.*). Quantitative data that may be considered includes the "volatility and level of profitability" (*ibid.*: 3, para. 15) of a firm.

Discussion

There are different rating methodologies depending on the type of debt issuer: sovereign, sub-sovereign and corporate variants. The loophole common to all these methodologies is that they have an internal logic; they generate ratings that suffer from a status quo bias and are not transformative in nature. Consider the financial crisis, which was an endogenous shock to the system. The sovereign rating methodology includes the anticipation of the willingness, quality and timeliness of policies in reaction to a crisis situation. It has an inherent blind spot regarding the origins of a stress scenario: the methodology treats the stress scenario as an exogenous event. This methodological blind spot has contributed to the redefinition of the financial crisis into a crisis of sovereign debt (Mennillo 2016). Consequently, consolidating public budgets became the order of the day in light of the deterioration of many sovereigns' public finances. while reforming the regulatory framework of the global financial system to address the very cause of the crisis was not part of the rating prescriptions. This is unsurprising given that the GFC is treated as an exogenous shock in the methodology; it was not problematized in the first place.

The damage such a methodological blind spot can cause tends to materialize in times of crisis. A further example is that of climate change. If CRAs do not take climate risks sufficiently into account in their methodologies, this will have consequences. For example, corporate issuers that exacerbate global warming may be able to gain easier access to capital. If we think of municipalities that try to increase their resilience to climate risks, these "deserve better ratings and, just as importantly, municipalities that do not do so should be downgraded" (Harrington 2020). Depending on how CRAs deem investments such as innovative flood mitigation systems, municipalities can be rewarded or punished by financial markets. Therefore, how CRAs view climate change matters. They can play the role of enforcing the status quo or facilitating the transition to a low-carbon economy. The stakes are high. Given that the impact of climate change and ecological collapse is an (irreversible) ongoing process, it may already be too late to learn lessons.

Rating through the cycle

One of the CRAs' ambitions in their work is to rate "through the cycle" (TTC). Rating TTC stands for the CRAs' aspiration to adopt a long-term perspective for their creditworthiness assessments. They try not to be influenced by ad hoc developments that amount to meaningless noise. For example, Fitch uses estimates of *cyclically adjusted* budget balances as input for the sovereign rating in order to rate sovereigns consistently through time (Fitch Ratings 2018: 32).

Considering rating TTC, CRAs can be characterized as a stabilizing factor in the market, which also explains the popularity of ratings among investors (Stellinga 2019: 27). As ratings are less volatile than, for example, credit default swap (CDS) spreads, this shows that CRAs, in line with rating TTC, mitigate the market's risk perception in its volatility and excess. Paradoxically, what looks like rating through the cycle can actually be equated with the pro-cyclicality of ratings, conferring a sense of certainty (and complacency) in good times while laying the basis for excessive downgrades when crisis hits. In other words, because of the ambition of rating TTC, CRAs seem to be behind the curve, react too slowly and only follow the markets. There is a difficulty in living up to the ambition of a rating TTC approach and being timely at the same time. As an answer to manage this dilemma, CRAs have different types of rating actions in their toolkit.

Apart from actual rating downgrades or upgrades, CRAs can put a rating under review,[16] or change the rating outlook. A review indicates that a rating is under consideration for a change in the near term. Outlooks estimate the direction with which a rating is likely to move over the medium term, which is classed as a one- to two-year period (Moody's Investors Service 2020a: 30). In the event of reviews, "further information or analysis is needed to reach a decision on the need for a rating change or the magnitude of the potential change" (*ibid.*). Instead, outlooks reflect the financial and other trends that have not yet reached or been sustained at the level that can lead to a rating change but may do so if trends continue. In order to understand the difference between these different types of rating actions, we can look at an example from the realm of corporate issuers. In March 2020 Moody's placed the ratings of seven European automotive manufacturers under review for downgrade as a result of the disruption from the Covid-19 pandemic. The rationale for this rating action was the

> deteriorating global economic outlook, falling oil prices, and asset price declines are creating a severe and extensive credit shock across many sectors, regions and markets. The combined credit effects of these developments are unprecedented. The auto sector (and issuers within

other sectors that relay on the auto sector) has been one of the sectors most significantly affected by the shock given its sensitivity to consumer demand and sentiment.   (Moody's Investors Service 2020b: 1)

Apart from the pandemic, Moody's acknowledged "a number of longer-term challenges related to Environmental, Social and Governance factors and megatrends in the automotive industry" (*ibid.*: 2). Increasing environmental standards and other trends in the industry, such as autonomous driving and new market entrants, were going to require "sizeable investments over the coming years" (*ibid.*). Despite the need for long-term investment in R&D "to protect their business" (*ibid.*), the rating agency regarded that as a burden for cash flow generation and profits. For example, back in July 2019, the outlook for Daimler had been changed to negative because of "an increasingly difficult industry environment … with reduced unit sales expectations and continued economic and political uncertainties" (Moody's Investors Service 2019). A few months later, in December 2019, Moody's downgraded the company to A3 with a negative outlook. In June 2020 Moody finally confirmed the rating and abstained from downgrading the company further, while keeping the outlook negative.

In addition, CRAs publish reports and commentaries, which also demonstrates their efforts to think about the long term and develop different scenarios testifying to their ambition of rating TTC. For example, Fitch published a special report in the context of the independence referendum in Scotland in 2014, advancing the view that Scottish independence may have negative consequences for the UK rating as it would delay the United Kingdom's return to triple A, which it had lost previously. It would be in the United Kingdom's interest to manage the transition "carefully, avoiding financial dislocations" (Fitch Ratings 2014). Another example is the 2014 immigration referendum in Switzerland. This induced Moody's to issue a "special comment" warning that "limiting immigration is likely to affect the country's growth potential, wealth and overall economic strength" (Moody's Investors Service 2014). The announcement did not constitute an actual rating action but stated that the "initiative aiming to impose quotas limiting immigration into Switzerland is credit negative for the Swiss sovereign (Aaa stable) and Swiss banks".

The point is not whether Moody's or Fitch is right or whether the other agencies are wrong. Whether the agencies pursue any agenda with these reports is likewise not the point. The point is that CRAs shape actors' perceptions. Most importantly, by diffusing a specific view on Scottish independence or on immigration policy and its economic implications (whether one agrees or not), a CRA influences public opinion. Market participants, voters and policy-makers may anticipate a rating action if the referendum is translated into reality in either way, which, in turn, impacts behaviour and voting decisions.

It is important to acknowledge this type of discursive influence of the CRAs, even if it is of a subtle nature and not directly measurable. Particularly in the case of special reports or outlook changes, this structural power is even more at play, as actors anticipate rating changes and adjust their behaviour accordingly. This type of influence wielded by the CRAs is seldom acknowledged and often overlooked. One reason for this is that, as mentioned previously, structural power is subtle and hard to measure. A further reason is that the acknowledgement of the authority often depends on whether observers agree (or not) with the agencies' expressed views. Agreement with these views tends to corroborate a complacent blindness towards the CRAs' authority, whereas opposition to these views tends to point the finger at CRAs. Instead, regardless of whether we agree or not with CRAs on different matters and welcome their influence accordingly (or not) in public debates, we should acknowledge the CRAs' authority in the first place and scrutinize it accordingly.

The caveat of the invisible in the visible: reading between the lines

The publication of the rating methodologies should not distract from the fact that there are certain elements of the rating methodologies that are *necessarily* opaque. Therefore, the CRAs' publications should always be taken with a pinch of salt. There is an inherent contradiction between what rating is and what it is thought to be. Contrary to conventional wisdom, a rating is not a quantitative measurement of credit risk but a nominal opinion about creditworthiness. The letter grade symbol epitomizes the tension between rating as an objective figure and as a judgement. Being qualitative information in a quasi-quantitative dress, it conveys the impression of measurement. Ironically, CRAs' efforts to make the rating process more transparent have contributed to the perpetuation of this myth. Since rating is judgement and not a calculation of the probability of default, there is no rating formula that can be published in the first place. Ratings are not repeatable, so no formula exists that can be applied to retrace rating actions fully. As an example, the committee deliberation that precedes a rating decision is inherently a black box element of the rating methodology. The minutes of these meetings are not available to the public. Bruner & Abdelal (2005: 198), citing Bhatia (2002: 26–7), maintain that "the actual committee discussion remains the 'invisible ingredient in the ratings process' across the agencies".

A transparency gap is an inherent property of judgement, which automatically puts a limit on CRAs' endeavours to be transparent. This is independent of whether qualitative or quantitative data is used (Moody's Investors Service 2002: 5):

[Q]ualitative and judgemental aspects are unavoidable even in the inter-pretation of quantitative indicators. Every measure we look at ... is the result of a complex interaction of economic, political and social forces as reflected in the policy parameters. Consequently, sovereign risk analysis is an interdisciplinary activity in which the quantitative analytical skills of the analysts must be combined with sensitivity to historical, political and cultural factors that do not easily lend themselves to quantification.

In the end, the mission impossible of measuring creditworthiness constitutes the *raison d'être* of the credit rating industry. There will always be a lack of trans-parency in terms of how quantitative and qualitative factors are accommodated and synthesized (Paudyn 2013: 808), despite efforts to do otherwise. Indeed, in the aftermath of the financial crisis, Moody's revised its sovereign rating methodology to reveal "how key quantitative and qualitative risk factors map to specific rating outcomes", and how "factor scores are combined to jointly deter-mine a scorecard-indicated rating range" (Moody's Investors Service 2013a). The updated methodology also displays information about the weights for each factor and sub-factor in the scorecard, whereby the latter are explicitly indicated as percentages, while the former are not. These weights are described as "an approximation of their importance for rating decisions, but actual importance may vary significantly" (Moody's Investors Service 2018a: 1). Moody's concedes that in particular circumstances the "weighting of a particular factor will be sub-stantially different from the weighting suggested by the scorecard" (*ibid.*: 28). As mentioned above, the methodology has a self-referential logic that legitimizes both rating action and inaction.

Furthermore, in the particular case of sovereign ratings, the very definition poses serious challenges to expectations of transparency and verifiability. Even though economic fundamentals can be proxies for the ability of a sovereign to repay its debt obligations, the prediction of the willingness to do so is, to the best of one's knowledge, conjecture. It is unclear whether there is a general rule of how the two aspects of the definition are amalgamated with each other or whether this occurs on a case-by-case basis. In the CRAs' defence, the two aspects may be difficult to disentangle. A preconceived notion of a sovereign's ability may colour the judgement about its willingness, and vice versa. Moreover, both are interrelated, influencing each other. A sovereign's willingness impacts its ability, and the other way round. In practice, it is hardly feasible to operation-alize these two aspects independently of each other. In other words, absolute transparency is unachievable.

Scholars and practitioners alike have suggested opening up the methodological black box, which is "only dimly understood notwithstanding the major agencies' publications on ratings criteria" (Bruner & Abdelal 2005: 212). "Contents" should be scrutinized, the "extent of uncertainty reduction" should be made explicit and "ideological biases" opened for discussion (*ibid.*). But, as we have seen above, such legitimate requests have their limitations because of the rating's nature as judgement, which contradicts the ideal of objective verifiability.

Apart from that, another reason why the procedure of the rating process cannot be fully revealed is that it would destroy the CRAs' business case (this also holds true for the hypothetical scenario if ratings were a pure technical exercise devoid of judgement). For example, restrictive access policies on the agencies' websites are reminiscent of the fact that CRAs aim to protect their intellectual property rights. As a case in point, Moody's updated sovereign rating methodology is accessible only for subscribers. In the case of corporate ratings, data that is confidentially shared with the agencies cannot be fully published, as this would clash with the interests of the issuers, who are the agencies' clients. The much-heralded value of transparency contrasts with CRAs' direct economic interests.

Nevertheless, in the wake of the GFC, CRAs have shown a concerted effort to be more transparent and to ensure that their rating actions are traceable. Considering the increased public scrutiny following the harsh criticism CRAs faced in the aftermath of the crisis, it is no surprise that CRAs have been eager to demonstrate their willingness to learn and improve by publicizing their revisions and updates of rating methodologies. For example, having published more details about its scorecard in 2013, Moody's continued to update its sovereign rating methodology in 2016 and in 2018. The reason for the latter update was a change in the World Economic Forum's approach and scoring scale for its Global Competitiveness Index (GCI). The GCI serves as an indicator for growth dynamics, which is a sub-factor for economic strength, one of the four main factors of assessment in Moody's sovereign rating methodology.[17]

These actions show how CRAs have been subject to increased pressure to legitimize themselves. According to a former senior analyst at Moody's, William Harrington, "recent attempts to reform itself [Moody's] are nothing more than a pretty-looking PR campaign" to restore its reputation (Blodget 2011). Similarly, the transparency-enhancing measures taken since the GFC are a way to invalidate criticism that can be damaging to the CRAs' reputation. Taking into account the limits of this transparency offensive, the agencies are facing a dilemma, which cannot be easily resolved. More importantly, the invisible elements of the rating process are – some would say paradoxically – at the core of the CRAs' authority. Consequently, the efforts to preserve the agencies' reputation through transparency-enhancing measures are a double-edged sword. They are, to a certain extent, protecting and undermining the agencies' authority at one and the same time.

3

THE USE OF RATINGS

Issuers, investors and intermediaries

What purposes do ratings fulfil in today's financial markets? Who uses credit ratings and what do they use them for? In order to understand the role of CRAs in contemporary finance, we need to consider the different perspectives of the consumer of ratings. From the perspective of the issuer, having a rating enables the issuer to have access to capital markets in the first place. It expands "the pool of investors and available capital",[1] implying a diversification of funding resources. This is in contrast to the situation when an issuer borrows money from a bank to refinance itself. Resorting to capital markets to access credit means that an issuer faces a myriad of potential investors, instead of depending on only one or a limited number of financial institutions to take out a loan. This may sound more beneficial for the issuer than it actually is, however. Admittedly, the dependence on banks for funding is significantly reduced. At the same time, a new dependence is created. With the pervasiveness of rating, issuers now depend heavily on the judgement of a few credit rating agencies to gain access to capital and secure favourable funding conditions. According to S&P,[2] the issuer uses ratings to "optimize the cost of funding"; having a rating from the Big Three allows debt issuers to refinance themselves on capital markets at a lower cost. The rating signals whether an issuer is creditworthy, reflecting a price tag of credit risk to investors. This knowledge reduces perceived uncertainty, and thus reduces the risk premium issuers have to pay on financial markets.

From the perspective of investors, ratings represent a "third-party opinion of credit quality".[3] CRAs regard their ratings as supplementary to the investors' own credit analysis. Legally speaking, a rating does not exempt investors from due diligence; it is not an investment recommendation. To put it bluntly, investors are ultimately responsible for their own choices. Furthermore, ratings create comparability across asset classes, geographies and peers, helping investors to make informed decisions. This implies that different type of issuers compete for funding; a nation state competes for funding with its peers as well as with private companies. Government bonds vie with corporate bonds for investor confidence.

Moreover, investors can use ratings as investment thresholds for credit risk and as investment guidelines. This kind of rating reliance is often not mandated by regulations, but occurs voluntarily. This voluntary use as guidance on an investment standard is emblematic of the embeddedness of ratings in market conventions. When a critical number of investors, including large institutional investors such as pension funds, use ratings as an investment guide, then the credit risk perception of bond issuers is harmonized across the board and rating actions become highly consequential in steering capital allocation. Rating changes can induce homogeneous and mechanistic market responses. This is highly problematic for a variety of reasons. For example, when a bond loses its investment-grade status, it often loses its eligibility as an asset to be held by institutional investors who incorporate ratings voluntarily in their investment guidelines. If lots of investors simultaneously sell the bond of that particular issuer, because the rating is the main investment standard, this will further aggravate the refinancing situation of this issuer. In other words, if ratings fulfil the role of investment guidelines and are adopted by a majority of investors, then this contributes to the pro-cyclicality of ratings. Such a systematic use of ratings contrasts sharply with the idea that, legally, it is supposed to be only an add-on to the investor's own credit analysis. In reality, it is the other way around.

Apart from their relevance for issuers and investors, ratings hold a certain usefulness for financial intermediaries. They can serve to benchmark the relative credit risk of different debt issues. When intermediaries are involved in structuring an individual debt issue for their clients, the rating acts as an indication for its initial pricing. Ratings determine the interest rates of a bond, and the latter are inversely related to the price of a bond. Ratings also facilitate processes of securitization; when financial institutions securitize or package assets into structured finance instruments, the rating of these assets helps to market the created financial products to investors (does this ring a bell?).

Not only is the use of ratings for credit risk assessment common among private or institutional investors, but their systematic importance is reflected by both the private *and* public regulatory reliance on credit ratings. Public institutions such as central banks, regulatory authorities and development agencies use ratings for credit risk management and as investment standards as well. The collateral framework of the ECB and the "standardized approach" of the Basel regime illustrate this point.

The collateral framework of the European Central Bank

When financial institutions want to pledge financial assets as collateral at the ECB to refinance themselves, these assets have to fulfil high credit standards. The credit standards are specified in the Eurosystem credit assessment framework. The ECAF "defines the procedures, rules and techniques which ensure that the Eurosystem requirement of high credit standards for all eligible assets is met" (ECB 2013: 36). It takes into account credit assessment information from credit assessment systems belonging to one of three sources:[4]

- external credit assessment institutions (ECAIs)
- national central banks' in-house credit assessment systems (ICASs)
- counterparties' internal ratings-based (IRB) systems

Although the ECB's collateral framework draws on multiple sources for credit assessment, this should not belie the fact that, depending on the type of collateral, only certain methods of credit assessment are applicable. ICASs and IRBs are credit assessment systems that are mainly used for the credit assessment of non-marketable assets. Examples of non-marketable assets that are eligible as collateral in the ECB general framework are fixed-term deposits from eligible counterparties, credit claims and non-marketable retail mortgage-backed debt instruments (RMBDs).[5]

For marketable assets such as central government debt instruments (sovereign bonds), ECB debt certificates, debt instruments issued by central banks, local and regional government debt instruments, supranational debt instruments, covered bank bonds, credit institutions debt instruments, debt instruments issued by corporate and other issuers, and asset-backed securities,[6] credit assessment is based on the ECAIs. The accepted external credit assessment institutions in the standard collateral framework of the Eurosystem consist of the Big Three and the largest Canadian credit rating agency, DBRS Morningstar.

Credit ratings are made comparable by means of the Eurosystem's harmonized rating scale, which consists of five credit quality steps. Every step is translated into the familiar credit ratings and thresholds. The external rating opinion delivers the content of the rule. As an overview, Table 3.1 shows how the ECB maps its credit quality steps onto the CRAs' rating scales (ECB 2014: 30).[7]

The credit rating, de facto, does the job of credit risk assessment. The ECB's collateral framework delegates the authority to determine safe collateral to the CRAs. This is not to say that the ECB trusts the ECAIs blindly. The fact that ECAIs play such a prominent role in the Eurosystem credit assessment framework obliges the central bank, for accountability reasons alone deriving from the regulatory delegation, to monitor the work of the ECAIs closely. Apart from

Table 3.1 The credit quality steps of the European Central Bank

ECAI	Credit quality steps (CQSs)				
	CQS1	CQS2	CQS3	CQS4	CQS5
DBRS Morningstar	AAA/AAH/AA/ AAL	AH/A/AL	BBBH/BBB/BBBL	BBH	BB
Fitch Ratings	AAA/AA+/AA/ AA−	A+/A/A−	BBB+/BBB/BBB−	BB+	BB
Moody's	Aaa/Aa1/Aa2/Aa3	A1/A2/A3	Baa1/Baa2/Baa3	Ba1	Ba2
Standard & Poor's	AAA/AA+/AA/AA−	A+/A/A−	BBB+/BBB/BBB−	BB+	BB

having to comply with the general acceptance criteria for ECAIs, CRAs are also subject to a performance-monitoring process.[8] Regardless of these efforts, it remains a matter of fact that external ratings represent the exclusive benchmark for the Eurosystem's minimum requirements for high credit standards. Furthermore, the harmonized rating scale with its credit quality steps is used not only for determining collateral eligibility standards but also for defining the levels of valuation haircuts, a further risk control measure of the ECB that is applied to eligible marketable assets. Likewise, eligibility for asset purchasing programmes and other monetary policy operations with underlying assets are based on the harmonized rating scale, and thus on CRA ratings. For example, in the ECB's expanded asset purchase programme of 2015, among others, the eligibility of securities was conditioned by "a first best credit assessment from an external credit assessment institution of at least [credit quality step 3] for the issuer or the guarantor" (ECB 2015).

The need to translate credit risk assessment frameworks and risk control measures into CRA rating language shows how constitutive of creditworthiness credit ratings are. Meaning is made of the credit quality steps by means of CRA ratings. Despite the ECB's efforts to regularly review the harmonized scale and the haircut category assignments, as long as adjustments are made in reference to the CRA ratings in order to be intelligible, the epistemic authority for assessing creditworthiness remains attributed to the CRAs.

The Eurosystem explicitly reserves the right to assess the credit standards on the basis of any information it may consider relevant. This implies that the discretionary power of the ECB to change the credit standards contributes to undermining and reinforcing the CRAs' authority at the same time. As Sinclair (1999: 165) puts it, the epistemic authority of CRAs in terms of creditworthiness is "constantly being both constructed and worn away". In the context of the euro crisis, the ECB's decisions to suspend the minimum rating requirements for certain government securities and to increase the haircuts for certain collateral are illustrative cases for the ambiguous effects of the ECB's collateral framework interventions on the CRAs' epistemic authority. In the case of credit standard relaxation, the ECB acts counter-cyclically and gains power to decide over what is safe and what qualifies as collateral, whereas the rating decreases in its ability to establish meaning. At the same time, the central bank's discretionary actions can be interpreted as acts of desperation, in the sense that the ECB accepts "everything". The latter reading implies that the CRAs continue to have definition power over what is considered as creditworthy and safe, while contributing to the credibility problem of the ECB.

In the following, I will look at the CRAs' sovereign rating actions in the cases of Ireland and Portugal. These actions preceded and contributed to the temporary counter-cyclical measures taken by the ECB with regard to the eligibility of marketable debt instruments issued or guaranteed by the Irish and the Portuguese governments in the midst of the euro crisis.[9] The ECB's decision to suspend the rating threshold for debt instruments of the Irish government was taken on 31 March 2011. On 2 February that year S&P had downgraded Ireland by one notch to A–, with a negative outlook (*Guardian* 2011). One day after the ECB's decision the S&P rating was lowered further, to BBB+, with a stable outlook, "putting the country on the same level as Thailand and the Bahamas" (Bloomberg 2011). Moody's had downgraded Ireland to Baa1 from Aa2, with a negative outlook, on 17 December 2010 (Moody's Investors Service 2010a), whereas Fitch had undertaken the downgrade from A+ to BBB+, with a stable outlook even earlier, on 9 December 2010. The ECB's suspension of the rating threshold in case of the Portugal, on 7 July 2011, was preceded by a downgrade by Moody's from Baa1 to Ba2, with a negative outlook two days beforehand. S&P had already downgraded Portugal to BBB–, with a negative outlook on 29 March 2011, whereas Fitch had downgraded the country from A– to BBB–, maintaining the rating watch at negative on 1 April 2011.[10] This left Portugal only one notch above the speculative grade (*Financial Times* 2011). As we can infer from the above cases, the effects of the ECB's counter-cyclical decisions of credit standard relaxation (or suspension) on the CRAs' epistemic authority are ambiguous.

By contrast, what can we infer from the ECB's pro-cyclical interventions? They unambiguously corroborate the CRAs' authority. An example to consider is the haircut increases that are equal to a tightening of the collateral standards. Just as S&P downgraded Greece to below investment-grade status on 27 April 2010, the ECB announced its introduction of "graduated haircuts on lower-quality assets" from January 2011 onwards (Gabor & Ban 2015: 13). The term "lower-quality assets" referred to sovereign bonds rated between BBB+ and BBB–. These assets incurred graduated haircuts in two steps: from January 2011 to July 2013, and then from July 2013 onwards. This decision had a pro-cyclical effect on low-rated government bonds used as collateral by financial institutions, making them less attractive and contributing to their sell-off.

Making the yields of the bonds spike, it exacerbated the refinancing conditions of the concerned sovereigns. Another example of the pro-cyclical character of the ECB haircut decisions is found in the treatment of higher-rated bonds. Bonds rated between AAA and AAA– enjoyed a decreased haircut from July 2013 onwards, which amounted to a relaxation of the collateral standards, thus increasing the demand for these bonds and favouring the refinancing possibilities for highly rated sovereigns. Through the CRAs' reliance on the eligibility criteria of the ECB's collateral framework, pro-cyclical behaviour by the central bank is, to a certain extent, predetermined.

Ultimately, the reliance on external CRA ratings in a collateral framework is likewise a rule-based policy, which lends itself to being transparent and anticipated by market participants. At the same time, it is notable that the ECB preserves the scope for manoeuvre for discretionary variation in its haircut framework, which defies transparency and a rule-based approach. There seems to be a remarkable trade-off between the transparency of the ECB's own collateral decisions and the autonomy of effective central bank responsiveness in times of destabilizing shocks. Less arbitrariness comes at the expense of increased reliance on third-party judgement about creditworthiness, especially at the moment when CRAs implement precipitous rating downgrades. With its contradictory signals in times of crisis, by acting simultaneously in both a pro- and a counter-cyclical way, the ECB obfuscates its ambition to acquire epistemic authority in terms of creditworthiness. Paradoxically, hesitancy in claiming this authority unambiguously and openly may preserve its scope for action to define what is safe and creditworthy without any reliance on external ratings.

The standardized approach for credit risk in the Basel regulatory framework

With the implementation of the Basel II Regulatory Accord, external credit ratings turned into regulatory tools to determine the capital requirements of banks. In order to increase the risk sensitivity of capital requirements compared to Basel I, under the standardized approach and the securitization ratings-based approach of Basel II capital requirements are determined according to the risk weights of banks' assets – i.e. credit exposures. The different risk categories are defined by CRA ratings, formally known as external ratings. Linking capital adequacy requirements to external ratings has been criticized for generating pro-cyclicality in terms of capital buffers in financial markets (Persaud 2008). Subjecting capital requirements to risk assessments and linking these to the CRAs' ratings in such a systematic way harmonize the market's risk perception. If perception is excessively optimistic, which is typical in times of economic boom, and reflected in high ratings, the overall capital buffer in the financial system decreases. In 2008 it was bluntly manifested to be too low.[11]

The regulatory use of ratings triggers mechanistic market responses especially in times of crises, when CRAs' comments, announcements, outlook changes and actual rating downgrades materialize in herd behaviour. These rating-induced cliff-edge effects stand in sharp contrast to the CRAs' mandate of mitigating the market's risk perception in its volatility and excess and to the CRAs' self-assigned ambition of rating through the cycle. For CRAs, the regulatory reliance on their ratings represents a blessing and a curse at one and the same time. On the one hand, it secures the pervasiveness of ratings in the financial system and the demand for the CRAs' opinions. On the other hand, the visible consequentiality of rating actions induced by the regulatory reliance invites criticism of their power. This puts CRAs in a defensive position. In this sense, from the CRAs' perspective, having the licence to issue a state-approved stamp or seal of creditworthiness can be regarded as both award and imposition.

As evidence for the increased rating activity during crises, Gaillard (2014: 128, tab. 3) shows the high frequency of sovereign rating actions between 2009 and 2013; the Big Three announced a total of 132 downgrades of eurozone countries during this period. Considering the fact that the regulatory incorporation of credit ratings was undertaken long before the crisis, during the period referred to as "Great Moderation", it is not surprising that policy-makers were probably not even aware of the epistemic authority they were underpinning. Downgrades of developed, highly industrialized countries were quite uncommon. Frequent rating actions were usually associated with emerging economies, especially in the context of the Asian financial crisis of 1997–99. The GFC and the sovereign debt crisis in Europe may have awakened their consciousness in this regard that market forces can question the sovereign creditworthiness of advanced economies as well.

The regulatory use of CRA ratings was originally driven and legitimized by existing market practices. Up to today CRA ratings have been used by market participants for a range of different purposes, whether for investment or risk management purposes or in private contracts, investment mandates, internal limits and collateral agreements (Financial Stability Board [FSB] 2014). In 2009 Jaime Caruana, former general manager of the Bank for International Settlements (BIS), stated in the context of the revisions of the Basel II Accord (Basel Committee on Banking Supervision [BCBS] 2009: 55, item 183): "One reason for using external ratings to assess capital requirements is that they provide a relatively standardised, harmonised, easy-to-understand, independent (third-party) measure that generally reflects the credit quality of a counterparty, issuer or investment product."

Efforts after the global financial crisis to remove references to external ratings in the standardized approach did not succeed. Basel III, the regulatory framework for internationally active banks that was developed as a response to the GFC, still contains the reliance on CRA ratings in its standardized approach for credit risk.[12] In discussions about the so-called Basel IV proposal, which aims to revise the existing standardized approach, strong opposition by the finance industry has revealed the market participants' preference for maintaining the status quo and keeping external CRA ratings in the regulatory frameworks (Verma 2015). When policy-makers follow the market's preference and reproduce market practice by relying on CRA ratings, then reducing the CRAs' authority to being a state *fiat* construct, as claimed by the "regulatory licence hypothesis", is obviously too simplistic. At the same time, one cannot dismiss the view that the regulatory use of credit ratings in the context of the Basel Accord reinforced the CRAs' epistemic authority. This acknowledgment of the merits of the regulatory licence hypothesis has straightforward implications in terms of the legitimacy of ratings as regulatory tools for credit risk management. A legitimization, which is based on the CRAs' expertise, creates tautological justifications. Since the regulatory use of ratings reinforced the CRAs' epistemic authority, the existing market practice cannot serve as evidence for the validity of the CRAs' expertise. In the end, this discussion also reveals that the search for the one single cause of the CRAs' authority is misleading, as multiple factors are at play.

Reflecting the unrepeatability of history, the counterfactual of what would have happened in the rating industry if ratings had not been used for regulatory purposes cannot be tested against empirical evidence. If the regulatory incorporation of ratings was conducive to the CRAs' market power and the pervasiveness of ratings (which it plausibly was), then the existing market practice has to be regarded as a co-product of the existing regulatory practice. This implies that an exit strategy according to the principle "let the market decide", as suggested by the CRAs themselves, is probably liable to perpetuate the status quo and to keep external CRA ratings in regulatory frameworks.

What are the alternatives to the regulatory use of ratings?

In the pre-GFC literature, calls for "rating-independent regulation" were accompanied by discussions about having greater institutional control of the CRAs, if ratings were to be kept as regulatory tools (Bruner & Abdelal 2005: 211). The simultaneous reliance on CRA ratings in regulations and the increased regulations of the CRA industry suggests that the latter path has been chosen, whereas rating-independent regulation would have implied a replacement of ratings with either more market-based measures or with a stronger reliance on internal ratings-based approaches.

As far as the replacement of ratings in regulations is concerned, not only is the spectrum of alternatives limited, because of unknown unknowns, but known alternatives also need to be considered carefully. For example, the reliance on market-based measures for credit risk regulation is hardly capable of eliminating the problems accompanying the use of external credit ratings, such as procyclicality and herd behaviour. Market-endogenous measures, such as credit default swap spreads, could even increase market volatility.

In addition, the replacement of external ratings by internal risk models has its downsides, especially for smaller banks. For larger banks, producing internal ratings is relatively affordable, whereas smaller competitors can save their resources if they can outsource creditworthiness assessment to a third party – namely to a CRA. This argument has often served as a rationale for keeping external CRA ratings in regulations in the first place. Lall (2012), for example, argues in favour of the incorporation of external ratings in the standardized approach of the Basel framework, as this would create a level playing field between large and small banks. The advanced internal ratings-based (A-IRB) approach, which is also part of the first pillar of the Basel II Accord regulating minimum capital requirements, would put large banks at a competitive advantage compared to smaller players. Another point of criticism of the A-IRB approach relates to its inherent incentive for banks to underestimate credit risk. In normal times banks tend to regard high capital adequacy requirements as indirect regulatory taxation. Consequently, in a counter-factual scenario, internal ratings would have an upward bias and be too optimistic, thus resulting in lower system-wide capital buffers compared with the scenario in which capital requirements are calculated on the basis of external ratings. It has to be noted, however, that this argument in favour of external ratings and against internal ratings used as regulatory tools cannot be supported by robust empirical evidence.

Is there no alternative to external CRA ratings?

Arguments that "there is no alternative" (TINA) to credit ratings in regulatory regimes for credit risk assessment often serve to legitimize the status quo. Is this actually accurate? Attempts after the GFC, induced by the Dodd–Frank Act in the United States, to end the regulatory hardwiring of ratings and remove references to ratings in financial market regulations are indicative of the spurious nature of the TINA argument (even though only a partial adoption of the provisions may prove otherwise).[13] Let us take a step back to explore the shortcomings of the TINA argument in greater depth.

The TINA perspective assumes that a common language of credit risk is indispensable in modern, disintermediated financial markets. For example, Scalet and

Kelly (2012: 478) argue that ratings are a public good that serve "the interests of the entire financial system", because of the reduction of transaction costs on the part of investors "who want information about debt instruments but may not have the resources or ability to assess public and non-public information about the firm or governments issuing the debt". From the desirability of decreasing information asymmetries and increasing transparency in financial markets, however, it does not automatically follow that this indicates the legitimacy of the status quo and the indispensability of credit ratings as a common language of risk that is also used by regulators. As discussed earlier, the notion of a common language of credit risk contradicts the original business idea of rating: to offer an independent third-party opinion about the creditworthiness of a borrowing entity to individual investors. The rating is not supposed to free investors or regulators from the scrutiny of the borrower and from their own due diligence. The rating offers orientation for the investment decision, but is not an investment recommendation.

As established in the introduction, ratings are opinions whose accuracy depends not on the precision, exactness or correctness of statements but on the diligence of the CRAs to offer an informed opinion according to the best of their knowledge. Nevertheless, the trope of the common language of credit risk implicitly assigns to the CRAs the role of defining the system of rules in terms of grammar, syntax and semantics. CRAs create the language of risk, and, at the same time, they are in charge of its presumptive accuracy. This concentration of roles erodes the legitimacy of the status quo, regardless of the desirability of the provision of a public good that can be commonly shared. The uniqueness of the language and the fact that CRA ratings are constitutive of creditworthiness undermine the legitimacy of credit ratings as the common language of risk, regardless of whether the language is considered to be indispensable.

A further shortcoming of the TINA argument that legitimizes the status quo is that it disguises the fact that TINA is a product of the CRAs' epistemic authority itself, as well as of the existing regulatory reliance on CRA ratings. To use an analogy: if you cultivate just one plant in your garden and then claim that different vegetation is impossible, your argument is valid only if your decision to focus on one plant produces irreversible consequences, which prevent other crops from growing. Given that, in social systems such as financial markets, claims of points of no return are often a question of political willingness and are therefore social constructions, it is hardly conceivable that the rules of the game are immutable to the extent that the externalities produced by the agencies' authority and the regulatory use of ratings are entirely irreversible. The transition phase, undoubtedly, will not be easy given the force of habit, the stickiness of market practice and the required adjustment costs. Without proactive support to develop alternatives to CRA ratings, market and regulatory practice are unlikely to change. In order to facilitate a turning point from the status quo and put an end to the TINA argument, the ground needs to be cultivated in such a way that viable alternatives *can* emerge.

Sticking to the TINA rhetoric underpins a status quo that creates the conditions that make TINA true. The self-justifying character of TINA blocks efforts to create feasible alternatives. The Financial Stability Board's initiative in the wake of the GFC shows the difficulty of doing so. In the end, the desirability of changing the status quo hinges critically on the assumption that sticking to the status quo is even more costly. The current market oligopoly, with its inherent potential of market power abuse, its epistemic authority and the related lack of other languages of credit risk, indicates the scale of the opportunity costs that have already been incurred.

The initiative of the Financial Stability Board to reduce the CRA reliance

The persistence of the status quo and the difficulty in changing it have become visible in the hesitant progress of the FSB initiative to promote regulation that relies less on CRA ratings. In the wake of the GFC a transnational consensus emerged that there is a need to eliminate the regulatory reliance on CRAs, which manifests itself in mechanistic market responses to CRAs' actions. As a result, the FSB, commissioned by the G-20 in the aftermath of the crisis to promote financial stability, was mandated to disempower the CRAs and thus end the regulatory reliance on external ratings.

In October 2010 the FSB released the "Principles for Reducing Reliance on CRA Ratings" (FSB 2010). The initiative brought about a series of reports monitoring the fulfilment of the commitments by national authorities (FSB 2012a, 2013, 2014). In its final peer review report, the FSB (2014: 1) pointed out the need for more work in order "to implement fully the agreed Roadmap". Success looked somewhat different, with "strengthening internal credit assessment capabilities" and "developing alternative measures of creditworthi- ness" posing the biggest challenges for the realization of the FSB principles (*ibid.*: 3). Furthermore, the "time required to build-up [*sic*] or enhance own credit risk assessment capabilities (especially for smaller entities) [was] hindering progress" (*ibid.*: 1).

In accordance with the roadmap, the FSB conceived of CRA ratings to be "an input, but no more than that, to the risk assessment process" (FSB 2012b: 24) by the end of 2015. Given the slow-paced implementation of the roadmap, this goal became increasingly unrealistic. In view of the variety of national action plans and the differences in member states' approaches across jurisdictions and financial sectors, the willingness to live up to the original resolutions of the ini- tiative faded away. Disagreement existed concerning the volume of measures to be taken, including the policy areas they were supposed to cover. In the end, the FSB was unable to overcome these differences among its members. In line with its moderator role, the main recommendation the FSB gave to national authorities was to enhance the dialogue with market participants in order to find alternatives in terms of creditworthiness assessment.

There is sufficient reason to presume that the FSB recognized its mission was impossible by starting to demand the possible. By 2014 the FSB had adopted a substitution strategy "light": first, to substitute the increasing reliance on internal ratings for the reliance on CRA external ratings; and, second, to advocate enhanced oversight of CRAs in accordance with the International Organization of Securities Commissions (IOSCO) code of conduct.[14] This combination of recommendations is a compromise, if not surrender, with respect to the initial resolutions of the initiative of 2010. Consequently, the FSB explicitly demanded improvements in transparency and competition among CRAs. It asked for more disclosure "about rating methodologies, rating performance, conflicts of interest, and other operational matters" (FSB 2013: 5). In other words, the FSB had to rely on standard setters such as IOSCO to "provide guidance to their members on steps to further discourage reliance on CRA ratings" (FSB 2012a: 4), even if this was not the core mission of the IOSCO.

It remains an open question as to whether the FSB went far enough with its agenda from the start. At the same time, it is debatable whether the FSB would have had the necessary influence to ask for more. In the progress report at the St Petersburg G-20 summit, its demand to reduce CRA reliance was amended with the demand for "increased oversight" (FSB 2013). If the watering down of the FSB's initiative was inevitable in the light of the deceleration and postponement by national authorities, it is not surprising that the FSB started to adopt rhetoric in which the increased regulation of CRAs would serve as a further substitute for plans to reduce the regulatory reliance on ratings.

In the end, the success of the FSB's efforts has depended largely on the determination of the Basel Committee on Banking Supervision, as the Basel regime remains the most compelling international driver behind the regulatory reliance on external ratings. The implementation of the revised standardized approach for credit risk, part of the so-called Basel IV framework, is scheduled for 2022. Its purpose is to improve the granularity and risk sensitivity of the standardized approach to determining capital requirements. The reliance on external ratings is still permitted under certain circumstances, both for the exposure to banks and for the exposure to corporates; credit ratings remain the primary basis for determining risk weights.

In December 2014 the BCBS (2014) published an early version of the consultative document entitled *Revisions to the Standardised Approach for Credit Risk*, which prescribed a removal of references to external ratings, in line with the FSB initiative. This proposal sparked intense opposition in the financial industry, such that "bankers hope the proposals will change beyond recognition before the final-rule stage" (Verma 2015). As a reaction to this, in its second consultative document, published in December 2015, the BCBS (2015: 1) conceded:

> Respondents expressed significant concerns, suggesting that the complete removal of references to ratings was unnecessary and undesirable … Acknowledging the limitations of removing all references to external ratings, the Committee proposes … to reintroduce external ratings, in a non-mechanistic manner, for exposures to banks and corporates.

Further research is required to analyse the reasons for the adherence to external ratings for regulatory purposes, and the role different states and private interests have played therein. In retrospect, timing seems critical. In order to bridge the gap between the demands of the FSB initiative and the market participants' preferences, the BCBS has reached a compromise between the two extremes of removing credit ratings completely and a mechanistic reliance on ratings. Whether additional due diligence requirements, "by developing a sufficiently granular non-ratings-based approach for jurisdictions that cannot or do not wish to rely on external credit ratings", are enough to reduce the mechanistic reliance on credit ratings in practice is a different story (BCBS 2017: 2). In the case of the United States, the adoption of the Dodd–Frank provisions regarding the "removal of statutory references to credit ratings" (section 939) and the "review of reliance on credit ratings" (section 939A) is still incomplete, as "a small set of references to credit ratings in Commission statutes, rules, and forms remain to be addressed".[15]

Wishful thinking: back to Basel I?

What would have happened if the regulatory reliance on CRA ratings belonged to history? Would global financial markets pose fewer systemic threats to the wealth and stability of whole nations? Even if the use of external ratings as the common language of credit risk was abolished, as long as the search for alternative languages of risk is ongoing the all-clear cannot be given. Considering the revisions to Basel III, the idea of risk-based capital standards is more than alive. The "simple concept of Basel I, to have some basic global capital standards, has been lost in an effort to over-engineer and micromanage at the global level the fine details of capital standards" (Verma 2015).

Given the experienced failures of the existing regulatory approaches to credit risk, it is tempting to ask: why not abandon the idea of delegated risk differentiation in regulation and return to Basel I? It certainly goes beyond the scope of this book to discuss this question thoroughly, but the fact that the crisis was not lesson enough to, at least, critically question the rationale of delegated, risk-sensitive regulation does seem striking. The taken-for-granted desirability of different languages of risk (whether internal or external ratings) as an indirect regulatory tool can be read as the continually "growing trend toward private ordering of traditionally public functions" (Schwarcz 2002: 3). What concerns financial regulation in general and the determination of capital requirements of banks in particular, the transition from Basel I to Basel II, can be categorized as a key moment of this trend; the creation of a quasi public-private partnership for credit risk regulation. The replacement of institutional variables based on volume to regulate capital requirements was done by the category of risk (Besedovsky 2012; Poon 2012). Importing risk as the main language to define these requirements implied the delegation of regulatory tasks to the models and entities capable of talking about risk – i.e. the CRAs. The seemingly irreversible reliance and dependence on these entities can be regarded as the price for welcoming a higher risk differentiation, an improved granularity and risk sensitivity in regulatory matters. It is notable that the ongoing trend of delegated risk regulation cannot be exclusively read as a simple unwillingness "to do the job" on the part of public authorities but also as a *zeitgeist* of the finance industry, in which static understandings of regulatory capital requirements became out of date, financial crises notwithstanding. Any perceived desirability and superiority of risk-sensitive measures – as opposed to non-risk-sensitive measures – for the regulation of credit risk and capital requirements outlived the GFC experience. This reveals an epistemological conviction in the ability to measure credit risk objectively. In this context, Porter (2014: 12) diagnoses a "continuity in the content of the rules" as symptomatic for the incremental character of the post-GFC transnational reform efforts, which can also be found in other areas of financial regulation.[16]

As we have learned in this chapter, the pervasiveness of ratings is co-constituted by private, institutional and public reliance on them. A critical amount of market participants take CRA ratings for granted to guide their investment decisions, without seriously questioning or contesting them. This de facto delegation of due diligence to the CRAs takes away the agency from the act of investing. It becomes irrelevant whether an individual investor agrees with the agencies' assessments. When ratings are incorporated as investment guidelines and used by public authorities for credit risk regulation, the rating ceases to be one under many opinions the investor can consider, as actually stated in the formal mission statement of CRAs and as should be the case de jure. The systematic reliance on CRA ratings by market participants contributes to the consequentiality and pro-cyclical effect of rating actions; ratings turn into a factor of systemic risk. To put it differently, if ratings were used as they are supposed to be used by investors, ratings would and could not move markets and capital flows. Neither the harmonization of credit risk perception nor herd behaviour would occur.

4

CREDIT RATING AGENCIES UNDER CRITICISM

"When life gives you lemons, make lemonade." This proverbial phrase is emblematic of the CRAs' relationship with criticism and financial crises. Whether it be the global financial crisis of 2008, the subsequent European sovereign debt crisis, the earlier Enron, Parmalat and WorldCom scandals or the Asian financial crisis of 1997–99, CRAs have demonstrated a puzzling resilience and crisis resistance. Their authority has proved to be immune to the public outrage generated by rating failures and to the harsh criticism of policy-makers, practitioners and scholars of different ideological traditions and camps. Undoubtedly, their survival can be explained by the CRAs' structural power and constitutive role in the financial system. But it has to be acknowledged that, in retrospect, the CRAs weathered the storm of criticism they faced extremely well. They were able to channel the accusations made against them productively, using them to their own advantage.

In the case of the Enron debacle, ratings were deemed to be insufficiently timely. CRAs responded by speeding up their information processing. In the wake of the GFC, CRAs indulged in a PR campaign after putting transparency measures in place to alleviate concerns about there being a fundamental transparency deficit in the industry – a view widely shared among practitioners, regulators, policy-makers and scholars. Embracing transparency, one of the much-heralded values in financial market discourses, enabled the CRAs to signal that their epistemic authority was still intact. Conservative ratings in the wake of the Asian financial crisis and the European sovereign debt crisis have also been interpreted as the CRAs' efforts to compensate for prior rating failures and to demonstrate their learning capacity. As a result of all these presumably strategic reactions to crises, CRAs succeeded in restoring their reputation and credibility.

The role of the CRAs in the GFC revived criticism, and the extent to which CRAs came under fire between 2008 and 2012 was unique. CRAs were scrutinized as never before – a fact demonstrated by the quantity of literature about CRAs that emerged in the aftermath of the crisis. The criticism was multifaceted and related to different characteristics of the rating business, and it surfaced at different moments during the crisis. Whether it was conflict of interest, the accusation of US home bias, lack of competition or the timeliness of ratings, the way in which the role of CRAs in the GFC was problematized in mainstream discourses has reinforced dominant ways of thinking about the CRAs and their authority in financial markets to the extent that the debate has reached an impasse.

Conflicts of interest

Distorted incentive structures accompanying the commodification of ratings have been identified as the main cause of the systematic rating misjudgements that led up to the GFC. The agencies' involvement in ancillary services of the securitization of structured financial products and the conflicts of interest related to the "issuer pays" business model resulted in a positive rating bias. The overly optimistic ratings of structured financial instruments, which were later revealed to be toxic assets, are regarded as one of the main causes of the GFC. This explanation for the crisis is derived from the toolbox of neoclassical economics, which emphasizes traditional microeconomic problems of incentive structures and asymmetric information (Dullien 2013). Bad incentives are the main cause of rating failure, given the assumption of rent-seeking behaviour by private firms (Bartels & Weder di Mauro 2013). "Rating inflation" is interpreted as "an attempt to attract issuers and increase fee revenues", and as an "unintended consequence" of the predominant business model, in which the same issuer whose bonds the CRA rates also pays the CRA for the rating (*ibid.*; Mathis, McAndrews & Rochet 2009). Furthermore, the cross-selling of consultancy services, in terms of the structuring and the securitization of financial products, has exacerbated conflicts of interest and positive rating bias (Amtenbrink & Heine 2013; de Haan & Amtenbrink 2011). The auxiliary consultancy services that issuers were offered by the CRAs also included *ex ante* suggestions on how to modify complex structured products in order to obtain a better rating. As a result, CRAs were complicit in enhancing the complexity of financial products and, thereafter, in overrating them. This confirms the statements of a former senior analyst at Moody's, William Harrington, that the conflicts of interest derived from the "issuer pays" business model "pervade every aspect of Moody's operations. [The] culture of conflict ... is so pervasive that it often renders Moody's ratings useless at best and harmful at worst" (Blodget 2011). As will be discussed in Chapter 5, the rating industry's regulatory reforms after the GFC were specifically aimed at increasing the separation requirements between the different CRA business units, requiring them to set up a "Chinese wall" between the company's marketing and the rating production. This type of regulatory response reveals a neoclassical analytical perspective in terms of problem identification (Dullien 2013). As incentive problems are deemed to be the main cause of the misrepresentation of credit risk and rating failure, the prevention of moral hazard is regarded as key for the quality of ratings.

Further conflicts of interest deemed to contribute to rating failure relate to the structure of ownership. Ratings are not issued independently but are set strategically, in order to maximize the shareholders' return on equity. In other words, CRAs act as the extended arm of their owners. According to popular literature on CRAs, the increase in the CRAs' profits during the crisis suggests such dynamics (see, for example, Rügemer 2012a, 2012b).

Considering the public good character of ratings, a reintroduction of the "investor pays" business model seems unlikely in the future. Apart from free-rider problems, ratings can suffer from other conflicts of interest in this scenario, such as a negative bias. CRAs could be excessively conservative when assessing bond issuers in order to please their customers – i.e. investors in this case. As we can see, regardless of which business model prevails, there is an inherent tension between rating quality and the commodification of rating. Because of this basic conflict of interest, rent-seeking behaviour comes at the expense of rating quality. At the same time, however, this does not mean that rent-seeking behaviour explains everything related to rating failure. Important as it is to consider incentive structures and their effects on rating quality, we should not limit ourselves to problematizing the CRAs' work in this way. A narrow perspective on conflicts of interest overemphasizes the logic of vested interests. It underestimates the factors outside the CRAs' control that can contribute to misjudgements, and it implicitly exaggerates the CRAs' agency.

One example to illustrate further causes of rating failure is sovereign ratings. As sovereign ratings are usually unsolicited, the conflict-of-interest logic does not apply. Sovereigns are typically not clients of CRAs and cannot go "rating shopping" (Bartels & Weder di Mauro 2013).[1] Consequently, unsolicited ratings should be the most unbiased ratings, because there is no incentive to underestimate (or over-estimate) risks. If we consider that unsolicited sovereign ratings are, for example, subject to a home bias, this suggests that conflicts of interest cannot explain every-thing related to rating failure. The notion that a negative bias in terms of sovereign ratings may occur beyond a logic of rent-seeking behaviour and material interests is drawn from a different epistemological toolbox, which emphasizes the role of ideas, beliefs and identity in shaping perceptions of creditworthiness.

The US home bias

One of the most prominent criticisms that CRAs face is related to their US-centric orientation and their apparent "lack of cultural awareness" (Bruner & Abdelal

2005: 203–4). The world's two largest CRAs, S&P and Moody's, are exclusively headquartered in the United States. The "epistemic predilections" of the United States are inferred from this geographical position and attributed to the CRAs (Sinclair 1999: 160). By "subjecting all [differently institutionalized forms of capitalism] to the expectations inherent in the American model", ratings as a "US phenomenon" can have "profound effects over time" (*ibid.*: 162). Countries that deviate from the CRAs' expectations tend to experience lower ratings. The disruptive adjustment processes that follow result in criticism of the CRAs.

The roots of the accusation of US home bias on the part of the CRAs were evident long before the GFC. During the Asian financial crisis CRAs were criticized for being unable to "really 'understand' Asian business practices" (Sinclair 2001: 443). Asian governments complained about the CRAs' sovereign downgrades, which they regarded as an illegitimate intrusion into their domestic political affairs and driven by US standards. Not only in terms of sovereign ratings, but also in the case of corporate ratings, CRAs have faced a wave of criticism because of their supposedly American worldview. In continental Europe, characteristics of the bank-based financial system in terms of accounting methods and financial ratios led to "[b]ad experiences with the Anglo-Saxon–oriented raters", which resulted in resentment among companies and financial institutions (Engelen 2004: 69; Bruner & Abdelal 2005: 204; see also Mennillo 2020: 244).

In addition, the European sovereign debt crisis in the wake of the GFC revived the narrative of the US home bias. Especially when the CRAs started downgrading European states at a high rate and frequency, complaints about the CRAs' US bias grew ever louder. For example, in 2011 German politicians of the governing coalition between the Christian Democratic Union and the Free Democratic Party criticized the CRAs for their seemingly politically biased perception. Such criticisms were often accompanied by calls for a European CRA to successfully challenge the hegemony of the US firms.

As CRAs are part of the US-centred global financial system and its institutional infrastructure, the CRAs' instinct for self-preservation would make them automatically advocates of American interests. The CRAs' political agenda would consist of maintaining the status quo and preserving the US dollar's role as the main global reserve currency. Accordingly, CRAs would have an interest in weakening the relative position of competing currencies for international reserve currency status and would downgrade other countries. Such a mercantilist reading is in line with granting the top rating to the CRAs' home country, preserving the US government's creditworthiness, regardless of its higher public indebtedness than other countries with a worse rating.

In order to save the euro from being a puppet of US interests, one can argue that there is a certain need for a European CRA. According to some economists the United States would, of course, have an interest in weakening the euro's position as a reserve currency. Indeed, Levey and Brown (2005) emphasize that the dominance of the US dollar is a key element for maintaining US hegemony. It is an open question as to the extent to which the CRAs in particular function as an extended arm of the US government. It is hardly feasible to provide robust evidence that sovereign downgrades happen intentionally in order to protect the strategic interests of the United States. Just because the United States benefits from rating decisions, there is no proof that there is an agenda behind sovereign ratings.

In the wake of the GFC, a range of empirical studies analysed whether sovereign ratings suffered from a home bias. For example, Vernazza, Nielsen & Gkionakis (2014) identify the eurozone periphery as the CRAs' "biggest casualty". Measured against economic fundamentals, affected countries were "on average rated almost five notches" too strictly between 2009 and 2011 (further empirical work on the CRAs' home bias has been carried out by Fuchs & Gehring 2017, 2015, 2013). In the aftermath of the financial crisis in particular, the Big Three gave European states excessively punitive sovereign ratings compared to the US sovereign rating (Buhse 2014). Fuchs and Gehring (2017) find empirical evidence that sovereign ratings are biased in favour of the respective home country, culturally more similar countries, and countries in which home country banks have a larger risk exposure. Remarkably, these findings of home bias apply not only to the Big Three but also to the smaller German agency Feri EuroRating Services and the Chinese rating agency Dagong, among others.

For many observers, the accusation of the agencies' US home bias amounts to a "fairy tale of the American conspiracy" (Hackhausen 2012). The exaggerated hostility towards the CRAs can be explained in the light of the series of downgrades of European sovereigns in the wake of the GFC, which many policy-makers had interpreted as an affront. Former internal market EU commissioner Michel Barnier criticized the CRAs for not considering many EU governments' unprecedented reform measures. In 2011 he even proposed a temporary ban on the issuing of sovereign ratings for euro countries in bailout talks (*Wall Street Journal* 2011). The policy-makers' discomfort drove accusations of CRAs' partiality and of US imperialism. It is a fact that the CRAs are private firms and formally not linked to the US government. Conspiracy theories are hard to falsify, however, and tend to persist.

With regard to criticism of sovereign ratings, "a curious dialectic in rating agency–state relations" (Sinclair 1999: 160) manifests itself. Sinclair (*ibid.*) notes that "when states are downgraded by the major global agencies they are often vocal in their denunciation of the judgements". When states tacitly enjoy and welcome their AAA status, thus acknowledging the validity of the CRAs' judgements, they lose credibility when they dislike the ratings, or even question their validity, when the tide turns. The political class loses credibility if it enjoys the benefits of sovereign ratings in good times and rejects them in bad times. A sovereign debt crisis is, therefore, not the ideal time to problematize the politics of sovereign ratings, since policy-makers are susceptible to the accusation of taking revenge on their judges.

Another argument calling the criticism of the CRAs' home bias into question is related to the overemphasis of vested interests. Sovereign rating downgrades may weaken the euro, from which the US dollar benefits, but this does not automatically imply that the US government or the CRAs are pursuing a political agenda and setting ratings intentionally. In line with the "synchronic-rationalist" mental framework of rating orthodoxy that Sinclair (2005: 70) developed, the CRAs' insistence on the cross-cultural nature of their sovereign ratings implies, by definition, the impossibility of having a US bias from their perspective. Unsurprisingly, CRAs, therefore, also dismiss criticism of US home bias as conspiracy theories.

The lack of competition

A prominent criticism of the rating industry relates to the oligopolistic market structure. Depending on how it is measured, the market share attributed to the Big Three varies between 90 per cent and 95 per cent, of which Fitch owns approximately 15 per cent, and the rest is divided more or less equally between S&P and Moody's. Since the degree of competition is low, market power abuse and rating failure are difficult to prevent. Based on their rent-seeking behaviour, CRAs would be tempted to manipulate the market in order to increase their profits. Insider information on pending rating changes, the strategic setting of ratings and a smart communication strategy offer many competitive advantages in this regard. For example, the CRAs' dominant market position would enable them to trigger stock market crashes from which they could benefit. From a moral hazard, rational choice perspective, the temptation to move markets in line with their concentration of market power cannot be ignored. According to Bartels and Weder di Mauro (2013), "these are ideal conditions for collusive behaviour". It is no surprise, therefore, that policy-makers across the ideological spectrum have called for the CRA oligopoly to be broken up in the wake of the GFC.

Is the promotion of competition in the rating market really the solution to preventing rating failure? Given that conflicts of interest obstruct rating quality, an increase in competition may exacerbate rating inflation. Under the "issuer pays" business model, the customer would have a wider spectrum of suppliers from which to choose, so that CRAs would be under more pressure to attract customers with their favourable ratings. Conversely, increased competition under the "investor pays" model might favour rating deflation in a situation in which CRAs compete to be the strictest in their assessments of debt issuers. In either case, the promotion of competition is unlikely to lead to a decrease in rating failure. The implemented policies of recognition aimed at safeguarding rating quality, such as the NRSRO status in the United States and the recognition of ECAIs by the ECB, also question the idea of breaking up the CRA oligopoly. If the concentration of market power were at the heart of rating failure, these policies would be counterproductive, as they support existing entry barriers to the rating market.

This is not to say that the CRAs' concentration of market shares implies that there is no competitive pressure in the rating market. At the same time, the CRAs' oligopoly can hardly be questioned considering the distribution of market shares. Nevertheless, in February 2015 the European Securities and Markets Authority, in charge of CRA regulation, launched a "call for evidence" of competition, choice and conflicts of interest in the CRA industry (ESMA 2015). The purpose of the call was to "collect information from market participants about the functioning of the credit rating industry and the evolution of the markets for structured finance instruments as required by Regulation 1060/2009 on credit rating agencies" (*ibid.*: 5). According to CRAs' statements, there is no problem of market concentration in their industry; "there is vigorous competition among CRAs in relation to price, quality and service" (Moody's Investors Service 2011: 13). Admittedly, these statements need to be taken with a pinch of salt, given the interests at stake for the CRAs to maintain their dominant market position. At the same time, it is noteworthy that the CRAs frame their oligopoly as a result of market competition (and not of market failure, unsurprisingly). Thereby, competition is not understood as a process characterized by many players but as an outcome that legitimizes the status quo.

Although the rating market consists of more than 80 players worldwide, the oligopoly of the Big Three seems persistent, which further suggests that a lack of competition is not the main cause of rating failure. Smaller agencies "are normally specialized in one country or sector and can survive only if they develop distinctive skills in their market niche" (Mattarocci 2014: 121). Moreover, there seems to be a win-win situation between smaller players and the CRAs. By building strategic alliances (*ibid.*: 38, tab. 3.3), small agencies can benefit in terms of the CRAs' reputation, whereas the CRAs can ensure their dominant market position.

The timeliness of ratings

CRAs have also been criticized for rating failure in terms of the timing of their ratings. During the subprime mortgage crisis in the United States and the sovereign debt crisis in Europe, downgrades happened too late (Gaillard 2014; Eijffinger 2012; Tichy 2011). The mainstream explanation for their deficient timing is that CRAs only follow the market and do not provide any relevant additional information for credit risk assessment. Critics are convinced that CRAs simply communicate information that is already known in the market (Tichy 2011). Metaphorically speaking, CRAs would act as delayed meteorologists. As the act of forecasting the weather would not impact the weather, CRAs announce *ex post* what everybody knows, without influencing the course of events. For this reason, a discussion on the CRAs' influence on markets would be meaningless. According to this logic, informational advantage is the main ingredient of influence. A lagged state of knowledge translates into a lack of influence. Similarly, CRAs themselves use the image of a thermometer to describe their work. They argue that ratings merely indicate the temperature of a fever and do not cause it, understating their impact on markets and revealing their ambiguous relationship with their own authority. As the *Süddeutsche Zeitung* (2011) put it in the wake of the sovereign debt crisis in Europe, nobody at Moody's wanted to know anything about power – even less talk about it.

The CRAs' influence on the market's perception of creditworthiness, and thus on the interest rates of bonds, cannot be grasped easily in econometric terms (as is often the case for econometrics and causality in general). Since causality is difficult to prove empirically, the dogmatic belief that CRAs do not matter establishes the orthodoxy. The belief in market efficiency assumes, by definition, that the market is faster at processing new information than the CRAs. This implies that the market has already priced in new information before the CRAs announce it. According to economic theory, therefore, CRAs are always late, and follow the market. To put it differently, to frame CRAs as delayed meteorologists corresponds to the idealized world of economic theory rather than to the CRAs' role in the reality of financial markets.

The orthodoxy that CRAs are always late and do not matter is, in part, relativized in the case of solicited corporate ratings. Since the issuer provides the CRA with insider information, the additional informational value of ratings explains why markets also follow the CRAs, and not the other way round. In the case of unsolicited sovereign ratings, however, the irrelevance of the rating information is assumed given that sovereign ratings are based on publicly available information. Sovereign ratings thus cannot matter in terms of the market's sovereign creditworthiness perception, as there is no informational added value.

In line with orthodoxy, the BIS (2011) circumvents the "Who follows whom?" question and underplays the CRAs' authority. It uses the expressions "sovereign risk" and "sovereign ratings" as equivalents, leaving it open as to whether investors' concerns about sovereign risk are subject to CRA ratings or whether investors form their opinions by themselves. At the beginning of the euro crisis, however, the IMF (2010: 103) commented on the market reactions to the CRA actions more explicitly, saying that "some of these negative rating changes appear to have surprised markets, particularly the scale of the change", which suggests that markets are, indeed, following CRAs.

Several aspects call into question the idea that CRAs can be equated with delayed weather forecasters. First, a weather forecaster is unable to influence meteorological events. CRAs, instead, are consequential and interact with the reality they are describing and the future they are trying to predict. When market participants follow CRAs, for example, because ratings are used as investment standards or as regulatory tools, then this implies that CRAs influence the perception of creditworthiness and thus investors' behaviour. This, in turn, influences the creditworthiness of debt issuers. To paraphrase the Thomas theorem: when people believe things to be real, they become real in their consequences. The fact that CRAs can trigger self-fulfilling prophecies, that they are performative, stands in stark contrast to the metaphor that CRAs are just forecasting the weather.

Second, the metaphor of the delayed weather forecasters contrasts with empirical evidence. For example, the erroneous French downgrade by S&P on 10 November 2011 represents in effect a quasi-controlled laboratory experiment, which illustrates how much CRAs matter (Reuters 2011a):

> Standard & Poor's mistakenly announced the downgrade of France's top credit rating on Thursday, frightening investors already anxious over Europe's worsening debt crisis. The erroneous alert, which S&P said was sent to some of its subscribers, fed concerns that Europe's debt problems had engulfed the region's second-largest economy. It contributed to the worst day for France's government bonds since before the euro was launched in 1999.

If CRAs only follow the market and ratings do not matter, why would the FSB launch an initiative to end the excessive reliance on ratings by public institutions and market participants in the form of voluntary investments standards? Furthermore, there is plenty of quantitative research that suggests empirical evidence for the effect of sovereign ratings on bond yields, and thus on the borrowing costs of a sovereign issuer (Afonso, Furceri & Gomes 2012; Kiff, Nowak & Schumacher 2012; Gärtner & Griesbach 2012; Gärtner, Griesbach & Jung 2011; Reisen & von Maltzan 1999; Cantor & Packer 1996).

Third, even if the market has all the information about economic fundamentals on which CRAs base their rating decisions, this does not exclude the market reacting to rating actions. Bruner and Abdelal (2005: 201) state that "their 'announcements' continue to have impact". A presumptive informational added value of rating is not the precondition for markets to react. Although sovereign ratings, in particular, are based on commonly known macroeconomic indicators, Cantor and Packer (1996: 49) find "evidence that the rating agencies' opinions independently affect market spreads". The CRAs have an additional effect on market perception, which cannot be linked to the concept of market information. Market information about economic fundamentals alone is not the whole story. It is the interpretation, the judgement of the market information by the CRAs, that accounts for the additional market move to rating actions. Precisely because CRAs use only public information as their basic data for sovereign ratings, it is the authoritative judgement of the CRAs that makes all the difference; their epistemic authority to fix meanings and define the dominant interpretation of creditworthiness that is intersubjectively accepted and acknowledged. Against this backdrop, it is perhaps unsurprising that the judgement dimension of rating is difficult to measure quantitatively.

Furthermore, the discursive elements that CRAs inject into the market before a rating decision also question the metaphor of the delayed weatherman (such as commentaries, reports, etc.). In the scholarly literature, credit default swap spreads compete with sovereign ratings in their function as metaphorical thermometers for investors' concerns about sovereign credit risk (Hull, Predescu & White 2004). By just comparing the concomitant deterioration of sovereign ratings with the increasing CDS spreads, the question of who follows whom cannot be answered satisfactorily. If the CDS spreads increase prior to a credit rating action, this is often taken as evidence that CRAs follow the market, and not vice versa. For example, in a panel discussion in 2012, a senior CRA manager used this argument to neutralize allegations that CRA drive markets by fuelling investors' concerns about sovereign creditworthiness. Although the use of CDS spreads as a proxy for concerns about creditworthiness is plausible, a comparison between CDS spreads and ratings neglects the discursive moves by the CRAs, starting with insider information, rumours, announcements, putting issuers "on watch" and outlook changes that shape the market's credit risk perception. Therefore, even if a widening of CDS spreads precedes the actual rating change, this is not a falsification of the CRAs' influence on markets. Discursive elements can be captured empirically via measurable changes in the risk premia and spreads, their origins not necessarily. In addition, empirical evidence suggests that CDS spreads also react to rating announcements, which raises further questions about the narrative of the delayed weather forecaster.

As mentioned above, the reproach that CRAs are always late draws on an implicit but strong belief in market efficiency – that the market knows everything in advance. CRAs can, therefore, at best only reproduce an existing level of knowledge. In this vein, a CRA's function is the one of a neutral observer, of a meteorologist, with no influence on the course of events. At the same time, the meteorology metaphor erroneously equates the CRAs' influence with an informational added value of rating, disregarding institutional factors such as the regulatory incorporation of ratings. Further, this perspective reveals a functionalist understanding of the rating business, which regards the reduction of information asymmetries as the main task of credit rating agencies. Strictly speaking, this is contrary to the idea of market efficiency. If we think this argument through to its logical end, there would actually be no demand and no market for rating services.

To sum up, the cause of the CRAs' influence goes beyond the question of the informational added value of ratings. The related question of who follows whom misses the fundamental point in terms of the CRAs' authority. We need to understand the relationship between CRAs and markets from an intersubjective perspective, which rejects the idea of a one-way determinism and, instead, links the CRAs' influence to aspects of reciprocity, reflexivity or – some would say – performativity of social reality. In line with their actual mission to mitigate the market's risk perception, the CRAs functions as a consensus machine on financial markets. If this machine falls into the trap of confirmation bias, fuelling preconceived notions, this can actually exacerbate market movements. "Intersubjective reflexivity" brings about circularity in creditors' and CRAs' worldviews or market beliefs and sentiments. These are reflected in the ratings, "which are themselves demanded by the agents affected by the ratings" (Abdelal & Blyth 2015: 3). The codifying of these views, norms and values thus constitutes the distinct feature of the CRAs' authority.

The CRA critique and the CRAs' authority

As we can infer from the CRA critique, there are two well-established orthodoxies, or extremes: the exaggeration of the agencies' authority on the one hand, and its denial on the other. Whereas accusations of being the long arm of the US government tend to overstate the agencies' authority, accusations of being too late and only following the market downplay it. In turn, accounts that relate the agencies' authority to a lack of competition in the market disregard the rationale of the rating industry altogether and are not really helpful in advancing our understanding of the CRAs' authority. It is important to remember that the CRAs' role is to provide centralized judgements about creditworthiness. Fixing meanings and interpretations imply the existence of only a few authoritative institutions. An unlimited number of rating agencies would counteract this role of the CRAs.

Distinct and, in parts, mutually exclusive though these different lines of criticism are, they lead to an impasse in the debate about the CRAs' authority, and, even worse, they corroborate blind spots. One example of such a blind spot is the political salience of the agencies' authority.[2] Consider the implications of sovereign ratings when states rely on international bond markets to satisfy their refinancing needs instead of imposing unpopular taxation on their citizens. National governments subject themselves to the judgement of CRAs to assess their creditworthiness and gain access to credit. States and public sector entities empower the CRAs to define the terms of orthodox economic and fiscal policy-making independently from the political system of each country. These private institutions determine how things should be done and award high ratings to compliant states accordingly, in a similar way to the teacher who judges students' performance according to a predefined set of standards. Sovereign ratings represent the case par excellence to study the politics of creditworthiness.

CRAs themselves concede that "the rating of sovereigns depends more on the art of political economy than on the science of econometrics" (Fitch Ratings 2002: 3–4). In the special case of sovereign ratings, CRAs invoke the positivist stance of "small n" to conceal judgement. The infeasibility of calculation is attributed to the "not enough n" problem, and not to its inherently judgemental nature. As there are not enough cases of sovereigns and sovereign defaults, there is no basis on which to calculate the probability of default. Especially in times of crises, when economic fundamentals are insufficient to explain the variation of sovereign ratings, ideational and contestable factors move centre stage. We learned from the previous chapters that rating is an admixture between quantitative and qualitative data anyway. The judgemental, inconclusive character of rating never fades away, which is why the distinction between the art of political economy and the science of econometrics is in fact spurious for all types of ratings. The interpretation of the data is what matters for the judgement, as the data does not speak for itself. Even though this is actually true for all ratings, in the case of sovereign ratings CRAs admit this openly.

The political impact of sovereign ratings has led a few observers to question the rationale as to why CRAs judge governments. As most sovereign ratings are issued without governments paying for them – they are unsolicited – profit maximization does not seem to be the major driver here. CRAs do not issue sovereign ratings to make money (at least directly). Reflecting the absence of the "issuer pays" business model, the political salience of the CRAs' authority is not to be found at the level of incentive structures. One obvious answer as to why CRAs engage in sovereign ratings relates to the importance of government bonds as an asset class in today's financial markets. According to CRAs' own statements, they publish sovereign ratings in order to provide a complimentary service to investors. There are deeper explanations, however, that relate to the type of authority CRAs wield, which should be discussed at this point as well.

Credit ratings are an object of interest for "the analysis of how international standards, which are often established by private actors, are practices of rule once they become accepted convention and interact with the actors and issues they were supposedly only neutrally measuring" (Guzzini 2010: 9). Sovereign ratings, for example, are not therefore a direct instrument of power that are used by the CRAs intentionally to force states to do what they otherwise would not do. This would be in line with a classical understanding of relational power. If we categorize the authority CRAs wield as a case of structural power, then this perspective helps us to reveal the origins of consent to tacitly accept the use of ratings as legitimate. Unquestioned practices as the use of ratings constitute the most effective power relations. Power resources do not have an intrinsic value, and do not exist in a social vacuum but are constituted by the value systems of the interacting parties, such as CRAs, investors, policy-makers, media and the general public. Sinclair (2005: 46) classifies CRAs as "embedded knowledge networks"; rating knowledge is "very much a social phenomenon". Therefore, as non-state actors, CRAs are not powerful per se, or omniscient when they rate states or corporations. The CRAs' structural power is based on the commonly and intersubjectively shared ideas, understandings and values regarding credit-worthiness. Guzzini (2010: 15) argues that a shared idea about what counts in world affairs "will strongly influence the status ... of particular actors".

It is not primarily the material influence to move markets, or their coercive force as the markets' gatekeepers, that empower CRAs but, rather, the shared ideas on which their work is based. If there is a consensus about the definition of sound fiscal policy in a given situation, this legitimizes the CRAs to demand certain reforms from countries and not others. At the same time, these reforms are legitimized through the practice of sovereign ratings. Thus, a perspective of structural power facilitates looking behind the scenes of the discourse of sovereign creditworthiness, which at first glance seems to be based solely on supposedly objective categories of economic data.

5
REGULATING THE CREDIT RATING AGENCIES

There have been various attempts to regulate the CRA industry in the United States, at the transnational level and by the European Union over recent decades. The global financial crisis of 2008 represents a turning point in these efforts, when there was a clear shift from a light-touch approach of self-regulation to a mandatory system of CRA supervision and regulation. As we will see, despite these reforms there are limits to addressing the rating problems encountered during the GFC.

US efforts

In the United States, the relationship between government regulation and CRAs first began as late as the 1970s. This happened indirectly through bond regulations of financial institutions. In 1975 the SEC introduced rule 15c3-1, also known as the net capital rule. Investors purchasing bonds rated in the investment-grade category by at least two nationally recognized statistical rating organizations (NRSROs) had to hold fewer reserves against these bonds. The SEC did not formally specify the eligibility criteria for NRSRO status. This led to an ambivalent constellation: Although regulators started to use credit ratings for regulatory purposes, CRAs themselves continued to be largely free of regulation (Hiss & Nagel 2014: 132).

In the wake of the Enron scandal in 2001, the United States led attempts to abandon the CRA self-regulation paradigm. CRAs were criticized for having missed Enron's towering accounting frauds. CRAs failed to fulfil their role as the market's watchdogs or "gatekeepers" (Coffee 2006). Moody's and S&P's downgraded Enron's credit rating below investment grade only four days before the company filed for bankruptcy on 2 December 2001 (Coffee 2011: 247).[1]

In hearings before the Committee on Governmental Affairs of the US Senate, invited experts suggested regulating the CRAs for the first time (Hiss & Nagel

2014: 133). These calls became louder during the course of the WorldCom scandal in 2002. As in the case of Enron, the CRAs were criticized for having failed to spot the breakdown and accounting frauds of the company in time. WorldCom filed for bankruptcy on 22 July 2002. Both Moody's and S&P's had downgraded the company below investment grade only two months beforehand (Langohr & Langohr 2008: 14).

Subsequently, the Sarbanes–Oxley Act of 2002 mandated the SEC to produce a "Report on the role and function of credit rating agencies in the operation of the securities market" (SEC 2003b).[2] Conflicts of interest, barriers to entry in the rating industry and impediments to rating quality were among the main issues of concern. In June 2003 the SEC made suggestions for how to codify, monitor and evaluate NRSRO status to address the problems identified by Sarbanes–Oxley (Sinclair 2005: 171). The proposals were criticized for not being sufficient to change the existing regulatory regime effectively, which consisted of the SEC's 1994 concept release and the 1997 rule proposal.[3]

In June 2005 the proposal of the Credit Rating Agency Duopoly Relief Act followed as the first legislative initiative to constrain the dominance of the CRAs' oligopoly. It mandated the SEC to reduce the barriers to entry to the NRSRO market, abolish the national recognition requirement and develop new eligibility criteria for registration (Langohr & Langohr 2008: 452). The existing NRSROs successfully lobbied against the bill, however, criticizing the SEC's new supervisory tasks as too intrusive and saying that they would prove counterproductive for the innovation and pace of the industry.

In September 2006 the US Congress passed the Credit Rating Agency Reform Act.[4] This act increased the influence of the SEC in regulating CRAs and established criteria for NRSRO recognition. Brummer and Loko (2014: 159) characterize the act as a "watered-down version" of the Credit Rating Agency Duopoly Relief Act. The Credit Rating Agency Reform Act conferred the statutory authority to the SEC to supervise the credit rating industry.[5] Effectively, the act put an end to the "old (and vague)" NRSRO system (*ibid.*: 160). It introduced an open registration procedure, with the intention of lowering barriers to entry into the oligopolistic rating market, which the NRSRO system had supposedly produced in the past. According to the new rules, a CRA becomes eligible to register with the SEC as an NRSRO if it fulfils the following requirements. First, it has to have been in business for at least three consecutive years before applying for registration. Second, it has to be able to provide information concerning rating procedures and methods, statistics on ratings performance and policies and procedures for handling conflicts of interest and non-public information (US Congress 2006: 2). The Reform Act's original aim of facilitating market access for new and smaller market players initially appeared to succeed, as the number of NRSROs increased from three to nine.[6] The oligopoly of the Big Three has continued, however, which suggests that the NRSRO system is not a decisive factor in contributing to the CRAs' authority.

The issue of conflicts of interest is one of the few areas in which the Credit Rating Agency Reform Act was more stringent than the Credit Rating Agency Duopoly Relief Act. For example, it demanded "a list of the 20 largest issuers or subscribers" of the CRAs (Langohr & Langohr 2008: 454). Furthermore, the SEC's final rule of 2007, based on the Credit Rating Agency Reform Act, required "that a NRSRO informs of any potential conflict of interest relating to the issuance of credit ratings" and obliges the company "to disclose the policies and procedures it establishes, maintains, and enforces to address and manage these conflicts" (*ibid.*: 458). Despite these efforts, however, the structural root of the conflicts of interest in the rating business remained unaddressed. The Credit Rating Agency Reform Act was silent on the dominant business model of "issuer pays".

The biggest difference between the two acts is the "limitation clause". Unlike the original idea of tougher CRA regulation, which emerged after the rating scandals, the limitation clause explicitly prohibits the SEC in its capacity as regulatory authority over CRAs from regulating the "substance of credit ratings or the procedures and methodologies by which any nationally recognized statistical rating organization determines credit ratings" (*ibid.*: 453–4). This concession made to the existing oligopoly invoked a great deal of criticism of the Credit Rating Agency Reform Act. As CRAs would publish their methodologies and rating criteria anyway to show that they do care about transparency, not least for PR reasons, the new rules would not really make a difference, and only, as it were, reinvent the wheel.

To sum up, notwithstanding the Credit Rating Agency Reform Act's actual mission "to improve ratings quality for the protection of investors and in the public interest by fostering accountability, transparency, and competition in the credit rating agency industry", it has not achieved a substantive change in the credit rating industry. Above all, it did not prevent the series of rating failures that have contributed to the GFC. One has to concede that the act was probably unable to develop its fullest potential. Only a year after its enactment the subprime crisis started to unfold. Considering that the act provided the basic elements of the post-GFC regulation in the United Sates, however, the legislation should have had enough time to bed down, having been in place for more than ten years now.

The main legislative body that emerged as a response to the global financial crisis in the United States was the Dodd–Frank Act of 2010, which contains only minor changes compared to the 2006 Reform Act (Hiss & Nagel 2014: 134). Dodd–Frank confers an expanded mandate and rule-making authority to the SEC to regulate NRSROs.[7] In addition to annual examinations of each NRSRO, an Office of Credit Ratings (OCR) was established, which assists the Commission in executing its responsibility for protecting investors, promoting capital formation, and maintaining fair, orderly, and efficient markets through the oversight of credit rating agencies registered with the Commission as ... "NRSROs." In support of this mission, OCR monitors the activities and conducts examinations of registered NRSROs to assess and promote compliance with statutory and Commission requirements.[8]

The new regulations prescribe enhanced disclosure requirements regarding rating methodology, procedures and the main assumptions and principles used to determine ratings; conflicts of interest; credit rating histories; and the performance of ratings. Concerning the governance of individual conflicts of interest, the law prohibits rating analysts from receiving "gifts, including entertainment, from the obligor being rated" (section 240.17g-5).[9] Further, the law stipulates a Chinese wall between those responsible for fee setting and negotiation and those for rating determination and methodologies.

The Dodd–Frank amendments to NRSRO rules also contain strengthened policies and procedures about rating methodologies, rating symbols and retrospective reviews. NRSROs have to establish internal controls, such as "periodic reviews or internal audits of rating rules to analyze whether analysts adhere to the [NRSRO's] procedures and methodologies" (section 240.17g-8). Amendments also include measures concerning the "standards of training, experience, and competence for credit analysts". With respect to asset-backed securities, the updated act prescribes certain certification procedures for providers of third-party due diligence services. Moreover, as discussed in Chapter 3, the Dodd–Frank Act requires the complete removal and replacement of regulatory references to ratings that set capital requirements and constrain asset holdings for financial institutions (Rivlin & Soroushian 2017). Further, Dodd–Frank has introduced (at least theoretically) a new liability regime that places CRAs on the same level as other market gatekeepers. At the moment, CRAs enjoy the privilege of being exempted from expert liability under section 11 of the Securities Act of 1933, which is in striking contrast to securities analysts, accountants and auditors (Brummer & Loko 2014: 166).[10] The Dodd–Frank Act puts an end to these protections:

Open[ing] the door to lawsuits wherever a CRA knowingly or recklessly fails to conduct what courts view to be a reasonable investigation of the rated security or where a CRA fails to obtain reasonable verification of relevant factual information from a competent party independent of the issuer or underwriter.

It has to be noted, however, that ending the liability exemption regime, per Dodd–Frank, is untenable. Regulatory authorities have continued to exempt credit rating agencies from expert liability even after the enactment of Dodd–Frank. Shortly after the provision took effect, in the summer 2010, CRAs were unwilling to give their consent to issuers to use their ratings in prospectuses or debt registration statements (Marandola & Sinclair 2017: 490). Taking the heat, the SEC issued a no-action letter on 23 November 2010 stating that no enforcement action would be taken "if an asset-backed issuer omits a rating disclosure newly required … and cites as the rationale the unwillingness of NRSROs to provide consent to being named as experts" (Gaillard & Harrington 2016: 47). The credit rating agencies' threat to boycott proved effective in fending off liability and preserving their status as opinion-issuing entities protected by first amendment rights under the US constitution (Mennillo & Sinclair 2019: 278).

Finally, Dodd–Frank, at least theoretically, also mandates the SEC to revise and change the CRAs' dominant business model. If the SEC does not succeed in finding an alternative, the SEC would have "to create a board that randomly assigns credit rating assignments to the NRSROs – an idea originally embodied in the Franken–Wicker Amendment" (Rivlin & Soroushian 2017: 4). The SEC neither came up with an alternative business model nor applied the random assignment model. Individual conflicts of interest at the analyst level are mitigated, but structural conflicts of interest in the industry continue to exist.

To conclude, the hesitant or lacking implementation of the Dodd–Frank provisions has sparked intense criticism. There are a number of caveats concerning the effectiveness of the new regulations. Rating analytics, liability aspects and the dominant business model have remained unaffected by the new regulations, albeit for different reasons.

Transnational efforts

At the transnational level, the International Organization of Securities Commissions (IOSCO) acquired its issue ownership in matters of CRA regulation in the wake of the Enron and WorldCom scandals. IOSCO is the global standard setter for securities markets regulation. According to IOSCO, the objectives and principles of securities regulation consist in "protecting investors, ensuring that securities markets are fair, efficient, and transparent, and reducing systemic risk" (IOSCO 2003a: 1). IOSCO conceives of CRAs as contributing "to achieving these objectives" by "offering informed, independent analyses and opinions" (*ibid.*).

In view of the scandals and the role that CRAs played therein, IOSCO issued the "IOSCO statement of principles regarding the activities of credit rating agencies" (*ibid.*). Even though they are not legally binding, the IOSCO's principles "were designed to be a useful tool for securities regulators, rating agencies and others wishing to articulate the terms and conditions under which CRAs operate and the manner in which opinions of CRAs should be used by market participants" (IOSCO 2004). The topics covered were the quality and integrity of the rating process, questions of independence and conflicts of interest, transparency as well as the timeliness of ratings disclosure and confidential information. The principles, for which different stakeholders "should strive" (IOSCO 2003b: 16), were based on the IOSCO report of 2003 (*ibid.*: 3):

> This report does not propose a preferred method for addressing CRA-related issues. Nor does this report endorse any particular regulatory approach jurisdictions may take regarding CRAs. Moreover, the report does not make judgements regarding the methodologies, approaches or business models CRAs may use. Rather, this report discusses certain key issues that securities regulators, CRAs and others may wish to consider when deliberating policy choices in this area. While some jurisdictions may decide to address the issues highlighted in this report through market mechanisms, others may decide to consider regulatory or other methods to address them.

Complaints about the practical implementation of the principles by commentators, including some CRAs, gave rise to a task force on CRAs chaired by the SEC (Hiss & Nagel 2014: 132). This led to the publication of IOSCO's "Code of conduct fundamentals for credit rating agencies" in 2004 (IOSCO 2004). As "a set of robust, practical measures", the code was supposed to be more specific and detailed than the principles in order to provide "a guide to and a framework for implementing the Principles' objectives" (*ibid.*: 2) in practice.

The code recommended that "CRAs should adopt, publish and adhere to" (*ibid.*: 4) certain measures in the quality and integrity of the rating process; the CRA independence and the avoidance of conflicts of interest; and CRA responsibilities to the investing public and issuers. For example, CRAs "should use rating methodologies that are rigorous, systematic, and, where possible, result in ratings that can be subjected to some form of objective validation based on historical experience" (*ibid.*) and a "CRA and its employees should deal fairly and honestly with issuers, investors, other market participants, and the public" (*ibid.*: 5). The "determination of a credit rating should be influenced only by factors relevant to the credit assessment" (*ibid.*: 6), and not, for example, by the anticipated economic or political consequences of a rating action.

IOSCO legitimizes its activities with the fact that "CRAs typically are subject to little formal regulation or oversight in most jurisdictions" (*ibid.*: 1), which reflects the dominant approach at the time of relying on the CRAs' self-regulation. In view of the "concerns ... raised regarding the manner in which CRAs protect the integrity of the rating process, ensure that investors and issuers are treated fairly, and safeguard confidential material information provided to them by issuers" (*ibid.*), the self-mandated mission of IOSCO is to improve how CRAs operate and how the opinions CRAs assign are used. The underlying understanding of CRAs and rating is that (*ibid.*: 5) "CRAs should endeavour to issue opinions that help reduce the asymmetry of information that exists between borrowers and debt and debt-like securities issuers, on one side, and lenders and the purchasers of debt and debt-like securities on the other". From this functionalist understanding it follows that transparency is regarded as an effective means to correct possible bias in ratings; the credit rating of an issuer "should not be affected by the existence of or potential for a business relationship between the CRA ... and the issuer ..., or the non-existence of such a relationship" (*ibid.*: 6). Through the disclosure of "compensation arrangements with rated entities" and "of actual and potential conflicts of interest" (*ibid.*: 7), CRAs would be disciplined.

It is an open secret that the code's lack of legal endorsement and absence of sanctioning mechanisms has reduced its impact. The code amounted to a quasi-declaration of intent. Although IOSCO recommended that "the elements contained in the Code Fundamentals should receive the full support of CRA management and be backed by thorough compliance and enforcement mechanisms" (*ibid.*: 3), the self-regulatory logic inherent in the voluntary character of the code undermined this recommendation in practice. The assumption that the incentive to maintain reputational capital would induce CRAs to follow the code proved to be erroneous. The fact that CRAs could not be held legally liable for deviating from the code greatly outweighed their presumptive self-interest in complying with it.

Although the IOSCO Code did not bring about the desired outcomes in practice, IOSCO's issue ownership over CRA regulation has been consequential. It gave IOSCO the first-mover advantage to shape the general mindset of how CRA regulation is supposed to be done. The code defined a non-binding transnational mode of CRA regulation as state of the art before the financial crisis, becoming the reference in the rating industry and the benchmark for CRAs to follow (Committee of European Securities Regulators [CESR] 2008a: 57–8). Despite – or, perhaps, precisely because of – the absence of legal enforcement mechanisms, substantive points of the IOSCO Code of 2004 set the global benchmark for the CRA regulations endorsed in the aftermath of the GFC and influenced the regulatory approaches of IOSCO's ordinary members accordingly (Hiss & Nagel 2014: 137).[11]

The GFC gave rise to several rounds of revisions of the IOSCO Code. The first round focused particularly on conflicts of interest related to the ratings of structured financial products. This problem gained in prominence during the subprime crisis. As mentioned above, issuers received advisory services by CRAs for the securitization of their financial products before getting ratings of these products by the same CRAs. Further revisions to the code included measures to enhance the quality and transparency of the rating process (*ibid.*: 136). Because national authorities put in place their own CRA regulations in the wake of the crisis, IOSCO had to make the code compatible with these countries' efforts in order to ensure that the code remained the "international standard for CRA self-governance" (IOSCO 2015b: 1). Additional revisions were based on "the experience of IOSCO members in supervising CRAs" and on the "work of the IOSCO Committee on Credit Rating Agencies, including the survey report describing the key risk controls established by CRAs to promote the integrity of the credit rating process and the procedures established to manage conflicts of interest" (*ibid.*: 1–2).

The final version of the code aims at enhancing the "integrity of the credit rating process, managing conflicts of interest, providing transparency, and safeguarding non-public information" (*ibid.*: 1). Moreover, it contains "measures regarding governance, training, and risk management" (*ibid.*), among others. The IOSCO Code still embodies a non-binding mode of CRA self-governance despite losing legitimacy since the financial crisis. It cannot be denied that the self-inscribed voluntary character of the code has undermined its own effectiveness. An alternative argument, however, is that the code's complicity in regulatory failure, in the past and at present, consists not only in the lack of enforcement of its provisions but also in the erroneous – purely functionalist – understanding of rating that the code has diffused.

EU efforts

Given that the Big Three are headquartered in the United States, this allowed European countries to de facto adopt the United States' CRA recognition without defining formal procedures of their own. Therefore, the European approach to CRA regulation during the pre-crisis years can be characterized as "free-riding on American regulatory efforts" (Sinclair 2013: 88). In other words, Hiss and Nagel (2014: 135) describe this as a light-touch approach of "wait and see".

Neither the Enron and WorldCom scandals in the United States nor the 2003 Parmalat balance sheet fraud in Europe were able to change the European Union's stance on CRA regulation. In the Parmalat scandal, S&P was criticized for a "gatekeeper failure" related to the concentrated ownership system paradigmatic for European companies (Coffee 2006: 16). The company filed for bankruptcy on

27 December 2003 (Langohr & Langohr 2008: 14). S&P did not withdraw all the ratings on Parmalat and related entities until 19 December.

In 2005 the Committee of European Securities Regulators took the IOSCO Code as the recommended guideline for the regulatory approach to rating "for the time being" (CESR 2005).[12] The CESR rejected the idea of "binding regulations" (Hiss & Nagel 2014: 134). The CESR argued that the IOSCO Code would suffice as the mode of CRA regulation since it would balance the interests of the different stakeholders affected by the rating process, such as CRAs, issuers and investors (CESR 2005). Following this recommendation, the European Commission concluded that "no new legislative initiative is considered necessary at this point" in addition to the IOSCO Code, "unless it becomes clear that compliance with EU rules or the Code is unsatisfactory and damaging EU capital markets" (European Commission 2006). This mode of CRA regulation is in line with the European Union's traditional "comply or explain" system of self-regulation, according to which CRAs have to disclose the cases of non-compliance with the IOSCO Code (Manaigo-Vekil 2012: 34). So much for the theory. As a result of the lack of enforcement mechanisms, as mentioned above, the effectiveness of this kind of approach left much to be desired.

It has to be added that the European Union indirectly tested a "CRA regulation through CRA registration" approach in the wake of the Basel II implementation in 2006. To recap the main points, compared to Basel I, the stance of Basel II – based on the standardized approach and the securitization ratings-based approach – was intended to increase the risk sensitivity of capital requirements using external credit ratings for determining risk weights of banks' credit exposures. The Capital Requirements Directive (CRD), which effectively implemented Basel II in the European Union, laid down recognition criteria for CRAs because of the regulatory role Basel II assigned to external ratings.[13] The competent supervisory authorities have to recognize a CRA as an external credit assessment institution (ECAI) in order for market participants to use the ECAI ratings for regulatory purposes. The Committee of European Banking Supervisors (CEBS 2006: 1) proposed guidelines for ECAI recognition under the CRD, underlining that "ECAI recognition for capital purposes does not in any way constitute a form of regulation of ECAIs or a form of licensing of rating agencies to do business in Europe. Its sole purpose is to provide a basis for capital requirement calculations". Unlike providing a regulatory framework for CRAs, CEBS intended (*ibid*.: 2) "to provide the basis for consistent decision-making across jurisdictions, enhance the single-market level playing field, and reduce administrative burdens for all participants, including potentially eligible ECAIs, institutions, and supervisory authorities". With the unfolding of the GFC, however, CRA regulation in the European Union began a new chapter. The European Commission turned away from the self-regulation paradigm based on voluntary compliance with the IOSCO Code. The European Securities and Markets Authority (ESMA), newly established in 2011, was granted exclusive and centralized supervisory powers over credit rating agencies.

The Economic and Financial Affairs Council (ECOFIN) roadmap facilitated the first step towards a turning point in the European stance on CRA regulation (Council of the European Union 2007a).[14] In October 2007 ministers "unanimously agreed with a set of conclusions to respond to the main weaknesses identified in the financial system" (European Commission 2008a: 5). The roadmap was "aimed at reviewing ... how to further improve transparency, valuation process and risk management in financial markets" (Council of the European Union 2007b: 7). It is interesting to note that there is no explicit mention of the CRAs in the initial documents attributed to the ECOFIN roadmap (Council of the European Union 2007a, 2007b). Later documents (e.g. Council of the European Union 2008: 15) formulate explicit tasks in relation to CRAs. In the early stages of the financial market turmoil the roadmap triggered a multitude of initiatives with a view to "restoring confidence and safeguard[ing] financial stability" (*ibid.*). The investigation of "structural market issues, such as the role played by credit rating agencies" became one of the main objectives among the lessons to be drawn from the crisis (European Commission 2008a: 6). The roadmap also induced the Commission "to address any relevant deficiencies" and examine "possible conflicts of interest in the rating process, transparency of rating methods, time-lags in rating reassessments and regulatory approval processes" (European Commission 2008b: 2).

Additionally, in autumn 2007 the European Commission requested advice from the Committee of European Securities Regulators and the European Securities Markets Expert Group (ESME) to assess the need for regulatory measures concerning the credit rating agencies' role in financial markets including structured finance (*ibid.*: 3). As a response, the CESR and ESME basically repeated their position of the past: no further European regulation of CRAs would be needed in the light of the CRAs' general compliance with the voluntary IOSCO Code (CESR 2008a, 2008b). Nevertheless, the European Commission, the European Parliament and the Council of the European Union all "ignored this advice" (Hiss & Nagel 2014: 134). Particularly "spurred" by the European Parliament (Quaglia 2013: 71), the European Commission no longer regarded "[s]elf-regulation based on voluntary compliance" with the IOSCO Code as "an adequate, reliable solution to the structural deficiencies of the business" (European Commission 2008b: 3).

In April 2009 the Commission welcomed the "respective approvals from the European Parliament and from the Council on the proposed Regulation on credit rating agencies" (European Commission 2009), paving the way for Regulation (EC) 1060/2009 (European Parliament, Council of the European

Union 2009), which provides the European legal framework for CRA regulation (Amtenbrink & de Haan 2009).[15] After starting its operations in 2011 ESMA received "exclusive supervisory power over CRAs", and is equipped with "a comprehensive and highly centralized set of regulatory controls involving detailed registration requirements and ongoing supervision" (Manaigo-Vekil 2012: 44). The latter entails the authority "to request information, to launch investigations, and to perform on-site inspections" at CRAs' premises (Quaglia 2013: 62). The existing rules were further strengthened under the lead of the European Commission, which in November 2011 "put forward proposals to reinforce the regulatory framework on credit rating agencies and deal with outstanding weaknesses" (European Commission 2013b). The reduction of the over-reliance on credit ratings, the improvement in the quality of sovereign ratings of EU member states, higher accountability on the part of CRAs for their actions, the reduction of conflicts of interest, the publication of ratings on the European Rating Platform and the promotion of competition were the regulatory goals the European Commission aspired to (European Commission 2013a).[16] With them, the European Union was criticized for going beyond the revisions to the IOSCO Code. The European Union's regulatory efforts risked "being seen as overly protectionist and out of step with international developments elsewhere, in particular the US" (McVea 2010: 6). Barducci and Fest (2011: 54) come to a different conclusion: that the new regulations would "only transfer already voluntarily applied provisions into binding regulations which reasonable acting credit rating agencies have already followed voluntarily".

An assessment of the CRA regulations enacted after the GFC

As the above account of CRA regulations has shown, competition and transparency have been touted as popular regulatory goals for some time.[17] Since the GFC there has also been an emphasis on reducing the over-reliance on credit ratings in market and regulatory practices. These goals reveal an underlying understanding of rating, which can be held accountable for the ineffectiveness of regulations.[18] Regulators continue to treat ratings as metrics and as a technical exercise instead of as a social fact. Consequently, regulations have a blind spot about the norms and ideas entrenched in ratings. The dominant understanding of rating influences a specific notion of rating failure and of how rating is supposed to work instead. Accordingly, it predetermines the spectrum of regulatory measures deemed as appropriate remedy. If the dominant understanding of rating is erroneous, then regulations resulting from it will necessarily be misdirected. Despite all changes in terms of the scope and intensity of CRA regulations, efforts risk ending up being superficial and costly cosmetic exercises with no meaningful impact on rating quality. Crucial aspects of rating, such as the business model, its public good character and rating analytics, remain unchanged.

Epitomized by the Big Three, the limited number of relevant rating suppliers suggests that the root of the industry's deficiencies is related to a lack of competition. Weak competition leads to poor analysis, as the rating agencies lack incentives to reinvest in their product. According to traditional economic theory, a major purpose of regulation is "to constrain the use of monopoly power and the prevention of serious distortions to competition" (Brunnermeier *et al.* 2009: 2). From this perspective, regulatory measures have to be aimed at increasing the degree of competition in order to activate competitive dynamics. These, in turn, are supposed to bring about a better market outcome – that is, better quality ratings. Striving for a level playing field and reducing entry barriers for smaller market players, noble though these goals may appear, will not automatically diminish the probability of rating failure and improve rating quality. The number of agencies designated with NRSRO status in the United States may have increased from three to nine, but the Big Three still hold more than 90 per cent of market share.

One regulatory lesson to draw from this is that fostering competition will not automatically lead to the desired ends. Accordingly, regulators should refrain from equating reputational entry barriers with a presumptive track record of the incumbent oligopoly. The idea that smaller agencies can catch up with the Big Three via, for example, "developing a track record score" is an empty promise (European Commission 2016: 8). A rating provides a centralized judgement about creditworthiness. By definition, this function can be fulfilled only with a limited number of rating suppliers. With an infinite number of suppliers, as perfect competition implies, the *raison d'être* of the industry would evaporate. Therefore, reputational entry barriers are not only the cause for the low degree of competition but have conditioned how rating has worked since its inception. The concentration of market shares is the inevitable consequence. Since reputation is inherently exclusive and not necessarily meritocratic, it favours the status quo.

Another dominant theme of CRA regulation is the idea that transparency can cure the flaws of the rating industry. Whether in the form of rating input- or output-oriented regulatory approaches, there is a common perception among regulators, policy-makers and scholars that there is a fundamental transparency deficit in the rating industry, which needs to be tackled. The United States has formalized registration to facilitate market access for new NRSRO candidates. As a quality-safeguarding mechanism, it has enhanced disclosure requirements for the registration process. In the wake of the GFC reform efforts, the European Union has also introduced a registration duty for CRAs. Against the backdrop that the rating failures of the past did not happen because of a shadow credit rating industry, it is questionable whether institutionalized registration and recognition procedures are the most effective tools to prevent a future rating fiasco.

Increased transparency requirements with regard to conflicts of interest have also been at the forefront of reforms. New regulations aim to mitigate the distorting impact of conflicts of interest on rating quality. Given that eliminating conflicts of interest altogether is out of reach under the current business model of "issuer pays", enhanced disclosure requirements are treated as an alternative means to address the issue. As these transparency and disclosure measures mainly affect the conflicts of interest at the individual analyst level, critics bemoan the fact that structural conflicts of interest in the industry continue to exist. The transparency requirements are "a distraction from the principal conflict of interest that distorts ratings, namely, the NRSROs' imperative to maximize revenues and earnings" (Gaillard & Harrington 2016: 52). Indeed, the European Commission (2016: 9) maintains that "none of the requirements related to conflicts of interest affected [CRAs and issuers] in a significant way, and as such they cannot be described as either positive or negative". Evidence is lacking to show that the disclosure provisions borne by issuers are effective. Rendering conflicts of interest more transparent does not mean that they cease to exist. Before the financial crisis, conflicts of interest in the rating industry were all but a secret for investors, issuers and regulators. The crisis happened, nonetheless.

Why should enhanced transparency make a difference, apart from having a symbolic meaning and a signalling effect? Regulators should keep in mind that symbolic transparency measures can also lead to adverse unintended consequences. For example, if investors discount a rating for its upward bias because of conflicts of interest, and issuers and CRAs anticipate such behaviour, ratings may become even more inflated. Another scenario is that CRAs react by being excessively strict and conservative in their assessments in order to compensate for suspicion that their ratings are inflated.

The attempt to boost rating quality by making conflicts of interest more transparent reveals a certain conception of rating failure. Rating failure is constructed as an inevitable consequence of the rent-seeking behaviour of (rational) profit-maximizing firms. CRAs are thus incentivized to please issuers more than investors, resulting in less rigorous ratings. Taking such behaviour for granted implies accepting conflicts of interest as a given. Transparency-enhancing measures are therefore not supposed to erase but to mitigate the distorting effects that conflicts of interest have on the quality of ratings. The social pressure to not give in to economic incentives *too much* is supposed to cushion the rent-seeking impulse.

Understanding rating failure and rating as such is not problematic. After all, no one can deny the conflicts of interest at work. Such a perspective becomes harmful, however, when it silences other causes of rating failure that go beyond an individualistic rational choice approach. For example, unsolicited sovereign ratings are not paid for by sovereign debt issuers, yet nevertheless rating failure occurs. Regulators should therefore refrain from perceiving every problem of rating as a problem of incentives and conflicts of interest, and, accordingly, not regard transparency as the panacea.

Increasing the transparency of the rating methodology, in order to make rating actions traceable, has also been a popular reform measure after the GFC. In addition, CRAs themselves have made tireless efforts to publicize their procedures and how they go about rating decisions, as a cursory glance at the CRA' websites reveals. Given the harsh criticism CRAs faced during the crisis, some described these efforts as a "pretty-looking PR campaign" to regain lost confidence and restore reputation, without having an actual effect on the agencies' practices (Blodget 2011).

The ideal of rating traceability and the notion that objectivity in terms of ratings is best achieved if it is the result of verifiable statistical models and algorithms (Roubini 2015) disclose a probabilistic understanding of rating, which misses reality for a number of related reasons. First, the rating process consists of an amalgamation of considerations regarding the willingness and ability to repay debt. Unlike mere calculation, qualitative and quantitative components are mixed in a way that prevents their later separation, as rating is the product of deliberation. Second, ratings necessarily involve judgement. Third, predicting the future involves high levels of uncertainty. Finally, if ratings were computable, there would be no market for CRA ratings. As long as the idea of making rating decisions traceable is nurtured by the probabilistic expectation that such measures can promote rating precision, correctness and absence of errors, enhanced transparency of the rating methodology will be ineffective in fostering rating quality and preventing rating failure.

Enhanced transparency in terms of rating performance indicators, such as the track record of the CRA, is a further output-oriented approach of regulation that increased in popularity after the GFC. For example, the European Union adopted such an approach with ESMA's setting up of a Central Rating Repository (CEREP) for publishing the rating activity statistics and rating performance statistics of credit rating agencies. A valid measurement of rating performance presupposes that the CRAs' predictions cannot interact with the social reality that ratings are trying to predict. Metaphorically speaking, the hit ratio of a meteorologist's predictions is a valid proxy for his or her capability, as a meteorologist cannot influence the weather that he or she is trying to predict. The idea that a transparent evaluation of the CRAs' track record is conducive to rating quality reveals a technical understanding of rating as a metric and disregards that rating is a social fact. It neglects how ratings can shape the social reality they are supposed to describe because of the CRAs' authority. A rating can become self-fulling and a factor of systemic instability. This has a straightforward implication for CRA regulation: the consequentiality of ratings, the impact of ratings on investors and issuers, invalidates a supposedly independent measurement of rating performance.

To conclude, advocates of output-based regulatory approaches have criticized the latest reforms for their excessive focus on input, process-based intervention. More output orientation would "create innovation-boosting consequences of rating failures, while keeping governments out of the kitchen" (Persaud 2009: 16). In contrast, proponents of input-based regulatory approaches emphasize the importance of opening up the black box of rating to increase rating quality and prevent rating failure. Whether one prefers a higher amount of transparency in the rating process or more output orientation on the part of the regulations, such measures share the fact that they draw from a functionalist understanding of CRAs as neutral, informational intermediators between borrowers and lenders that are supposed to decrease information asymmetries in financial markets. The underlying assumption is that objective knowledge about creditworthiness or credit risk pre-exists. Consequently, the regulators' task is to make sure that CRAs are able to express this unbiased view by silencing the different noises, such as conflicts of interest or bad practices, that are supposed to prevent the CRAs from doing so. The fact that the normativity of rating as judgement remains, even if absolute transparency is realized, is something that goes unnoticed in the different efforts to regulate the CRA industry across countries, transnationally and over time.

6

CREDIT RATING IN CHINA

As of July 2020 the Chinese corporate bond market had grown to become the second largest in the world, valued at $7.4 trillion, behind the United States at $10.9 trillion. The United States and China make up make up 45 per cent of the total global corporate bond market, in which 53 per cent ($21.5 trillion) of outstanding corporate bonds are issued by financial institutions. In the light of such empirical dynamics, it is imperative to look at credit rating in China.

A brief history

China's endeavour to create a more market-oriented financial system over the last 30 years predetermined, at least in the long run, that banks would no longer play their traditional role in financial intermediation and that a financial infrastructure would be needed in which CRAs fulfil a key role in the governance of capital flows. In recognition of the structural power of non-state actors, such as CRAs, in a financially globalized world, the Chinese authorities started to develop a domestic credit rating industry in the context of its own capital market development. In 1987 China took the first steps to establishing a credit rating industry by introducing new regulations on corporate bonds (Cousin 2007: 35). At the beginning of the 1990s corporate bond rating became the core business of the Chinese rating industry (Gras 2005: 32). As the former planning commission, the National Development and Reform Commission (NDRC), retained exclusive authority as the market's gatekeeper, Chinese CRAs had the symbolic function of creating the semblance of a developed capital market. Consequently, the factual influence of CRAs on bond issuers and investors was characterized as weak at the time (Kennedy 2008).

This began to be reversed only in the early 2000s, when the industry started to develop (Chen & Everling 2002). In 2002 the China Securities Regulatory Commission (CSRC) brought in comprehensive regulations for the CRA industry, including accreditation requirements (Kennedy 2008: 75). This was the same CSRC, preceded by the People's Bank of China (PBoC), that had since the late 1990s been the guiding force behind the creation of a fully fledged and functional credit rating industry following the American model. Indeed, China started to adopt international regulatory practices and standards by introducing rating-based financial regulation. As in the United States, Chinese CRAs have been granted regulatory licences; ratings are used as a regulatory requirement for bond issuance and investments (Gras 2005: 52–3). In this context, Kennedy (2008: 65) notes that the use of ratings as tools in financial regulation "may be the best barometer to measure the Chinese government's general stance towards private authority". Whether the advancement of a Chinese credit rating industry marks the transfer from state to private forms of authority in capital allocation in China's political economy, and is even a harbinger of the empowerment of non-state actors in Chinese state capitalism, remains to be seen. Sheng (2019: 400) concludes that "China's credit rating services have made progress in credit rating procedure, methodology and reporting, accompanying the rapid development of China's bond market in the last decade".

The major players

Today the Chinese credit rating industry is dominated by four major CRAs: Dagong Global Credit Rating, China Lianhe Credit Rating, Shanghai Brilliance Credit Rating and Investors Service and China Chengxin International Credit Rating (CCXI). These four agencies operate in the nationwide credit rating business and "have full licensing accredited by four government authorities (PBoC, CSRC, NDRC and CBIRC [China Banking and Insurance Regulatory Commission]) to provide rating services" (Sheng 2019: 393). The regulatory responsibilities of bond ratings are split between the PBoC on the interbank bond market and the CSRC on the exchange market (*ibid.*: 400). In addition to these major rating agencies, there are also about 68 smaller, domestic CRAs that operate locally in niche markets, specific sectors or industries. In most cases, local authorities or research institutions are founders of these companies (Cousin 2007: 35).

Market access policies prevented an oligopoly of the Big Three forming in China. Usually, the strategic alliances between local CRAs in other countries and the Big Three have served to perpetuate the status quo of the global rating market. Although the closed capital account in China kept international investors outside its financial market, foreign CRAs (i.e. the Big Three) were granted access to the Chinese market through the formation of joint ventures with domestic agencies. Moody's did so with China Chengxin in 2006, Fitch Ratings with China

Lianhe in 2007 and S&P with Shanghai Brilliance in 2008. China has developed its own, home-grown Chinese rating industry, capitalizing on the know-how, training and technology transfer by the Big Three through these joint ventures.

In the wake of the GFC, the major players in China's increasingly relevant domestic rating industry have made moves to break up the persistent oligopoly of the US Big Three. Most notably, Dagong, one of the largest CRAs, started issuing sovereign ratings in 2010 with the intention of challenging the hegemony of the Western institutions. Dagong covers up to 90 sovereigns, claiming a unique way of rating and presenting itself as a reformer of the international credit rating system. In August 2018, however, Dagong was banned from domestic Chinese operations in the corporate bond market because of misconduct, including the provision of consultation services to its clients and poor internal management and modelling practices, which contributed to excessively favourable ratings (Reuters 2019). In April 2019 a state-owned investment firm, China Reform Holdings, took a 58 per cent stake in Dagong Global Credit to assist in reorganizing the business. In November 2019 Dagong resumed all operations. The explicit link of one of the largest CRAs to the Chinese government may jeopardize its ambition to shift the authoritative centre of credit rating to the East, as discussed in the next section. For sovereign ratings in particular, independence from government is critical for acceptance of the impartiality of the agency's judgement and rating credibility.

Dagong's sovereign ratings: challenging the Big Three or just reinventing the wheel?

In order to challenge the hegemonic position of the American credit rating agencies, one of the largest Chinese credit rating agencies has advanced claims for narrative authority in the discourse of creditworthiness. Dagong claims to promulgate an alternative model of political and economic organization when assessing the creditworthiness of sovereigns that issue bonds on global capital markets, as the Big Three are often characterized as propagators of neoliberalism (Paudyn 2013).

Dagong Global Credit Rating Co., Ltd is a stand-alone Chinese CRA that has never had a contractual relationship with any of the Big Three. According to Dagong's chairman and founder, Guan Jianzhong, it is the company's "historic call" to relocate the world's centre of credit rating from the West to the East, "to create a professional, impartial, authoritative and influential credit rating agency" which is supposed to contribute to the "continual improvement of the financial market".[1]

Dagong was founded in 1994 on the joint approval of the PBoC and the former State Economic and Trade Commission. Its headquarters are in Beijing. Dagong employs approximately 600 analysts and staff and operates 34 branches domestically. It has launched two subsidiaries outside mainland China, in Europe and Hong Kong. This expansion has been interpreted as the "first Asian credit rating company to challenge US domination in the European credit rating business" (*China Daily* 2013).

Dagong issued its first sovereign credit rating report in July 2010 in the wake of the GFC. Since then it has issued sovereign ratings of more than 90 countries and regions. Dagong describes itself as "a globally-oriented" and "first non-western" CRA that, "[a]s the founder of sovereign credit rating criteria, … provide[s] the world with sovereign credit risk information" (Dagong Europe 2016). Dagong emphasizes that it has developed its own and original rating methodology (Dagong Hong Kong 2015), as if Dagong is trying to distinguish itself from its competitors, and especially from the Big Three. The extent to which references to the "Dagong credit theory" or "the establishment of the Chinese rating theory" are rhetoric or point to a truly new way of rating is an empirical question.

Indeed, the English version of Dagong's published sovereign rating methodology is reminiscent of those published by the American counterparts. What Dagong refers to as "economic strength" is equivalent to S&P's "economic score", "fiscal strength" corresponds to "fiscal score" and Dagong's "foreign exchange strength" corresponds largely to S&P's "external score". "Financial strength" corresponds roughly to S&P's "monetary score", even though Dagong splits financial strength into two categories, namely "development level of financial system" and "stability of financial system". The analysis of monetary policy is part of the former category. The latter category seems to have no equivalent in S&P's sovereign rating methodology.

At the same time, we should not overemphasize the similarities between Dagong and the Big Three in terms of sovereign rating methodologies. Compared to the three pages of Dagong's rating methodology in English, a glance at Dagong's Mandarin version, with its 52 pages, reveals that Dagong uses a different taxonomy (Dagong Global Credit Rating 2015). According to this elaborated document, the sovereign analysis consists of the following four factors: (a) the debt servicing environment; (b) wealth creation ability; (c) source(s) of debt service; and (d) solvency analysis. In part, they overlap with the categories listed in the English version, but there are aspects that are unique to Dagong's approach. Further research is required to compare systematically the rating methodologies of Dagong and the American oligopoly in order to determine the extent to which Dagong is really adopting a unique method of rating, or whether it is only reinventing the wheel.

On the occasion of the sovereign debt crisis in Europe, Dagong's chairman Guan Jianzhong commented on the supposedly "ideologically driven standards" of the CRAs' sovereign rating methodologies (*Tageszeitung* 2011, own translation). It would not be sensible to stylize an ideology as a benchmark for the determination of a sovereign's creditworthiness. The American CRAs would equate sovereign creditworthiness with the Western standards of liberal democracies. Deviation from this ideal type would inform the ordinal rating scale. For example, central bank independence, currency convertibility and the openness of the economy and of the financial sector would not be relevant factors that determine a country's creditworthiness. The Big Three would put too much emphasis on the willingness of a sovereign to repay its debt (which escapes measurement), at the cost of neglecting the sovereign's actual practical capability to repay its debt (which is usually measured by economic fundamentals).

Even though the published "Dagong sovereign credit rating methodology" includes the sovereign's "willingness" to repay debt in its definition of sovereign ratings (Dagong Hong Kong 2015), according to Guan's statements Dagong distances itself from this tricky task. The company would mainly focus on a country's capability to repay debt. Whatever is conducive to this capability scores positively in the rating, such as the policy effectiveness of the system on its economic management or the extent to which the financial sector serves the needs of the real economy.

It is questionable whether these aspects really correspond to an output-oriented capability approach, however. Rather, they reveal that it is in the eye of the beholder as to which aspects are deemed conducive to the practical capability of a sovereign to repay its debt. In short, the idea that rating can be exempt from ideological and normative considerations and follow a purely output-oriented approach is illusory.

This point is well illustrated with Dagong's downgrading of the United States from A to A–, with a negative outlook, in October 2013 (Reuters 2013a). According to Dagong, the United States would be in "a situation that cannot be substantially alleviated in the foreseeable future" (*ibid.*). Debt growth in the country would still outpace fiscal income and GDP. Despite a "last minute agreement in Congress", the United States would be "still approaching the verge of default crisis". At the time, the CRAs stuck to a relatively high US sovereign rating regardless of the turmoil in Congress accompanying the federal government shutdown in the absence of funding legislation and reflecting the debt ceiling debates. When Dagong downgraded the United States, in October 2013, Moody's rated the country Aaa with a stable outlook, Fitch AAA with a negative outlook and S&P AA– with a stable outlook (Reuters 2013b).[2] Guan seized this opportunity to blame the CRAs for having lost their professional ethics (*Süddeutsche Zeitung* 2013, own translation). The CRAs would function as an extended arm of the US government by indirectly approving the expansive monetary policy of the Federal Reserve with their favourable ratings. Dagong's opinion of the Federal Reserve's quantitative easing as a monetary policy response to the GFC demonstrates that what constitutes a "good" or "bad" monetary policy in a specific historical circumstance is a highly controversial issue. But raters, in the end, have to come up with a judgement about the prospects of a sovereign government being able and willing to repay its debt, despite existing ambiguities. In other words, because of the contingency of social reality, the politics of creditworthiness is inescapable.

As a pragmatic answer to the intricacies of the rating business, Dagong proposes a "Reform of the international credit rating system". As a representative of Chinese credit rating agencies, Dagong is pushing this reform and has mapped out guiding principles. Dagong identifies the current international credit rating system as "the source of the global credit crisis" (Dagong Global Credit Rating n.d.: 6). Therefore, Dagong promotes the establishment of an "international credit rating agency" that would be able to provide a platform on which the rating agencies of all countries could work together in order to guarantee the safety of the global credit system (*Tageszeitung* 2011).

Dysfunctionality in the rating market: causes and indicators

If we look at the current state of the rating market in China, it would be erroneous to assume that rating inflation is limited to a single institution. It affects the whole industry. Despite – or perhaps even *because* of – the multitude of players, rating inflation on the corporate bond markets testifies to the deficiencies of China's domestic rating industry. The corporate ratings of domestic agencies are deemed too favourable by market participants and international observers, conferring a false sense of certainty. Forty per cent are triple-A, which is "far above the global average" (*Financial Times* 2019b). By the end of June 2018 "97% of 1,744 Chinese bond issuers were rated with AA and above, of which 464 bond issuers obtained the highest rating" (Sheng 2019: 397). Being excessively optimistic and lacking differentiation, these ratings seem to misrepresent the credit risk of financial assets favouring a misallocation of credit.[3] As in the lead-up to the global financial crisis 2008, once the rating bubble bursts, the unsustainable debt levels will surface and translate into financial losses.

From a social constructivist point of view, the idea that ratings misrepresent credit risk is problematic. It implies that ratings deviate from an imagined true, correct or objective level. Ratings are social constructions, however. Such an analytical perspective assumes away the existence of an exogenously given rating that is supposed to be discovered by the CRAs if they only do their job properly. Once investors acknowledge the commonly shared, intersubjective interpretation of creditworthiness diffused by the authoritative agencies, ratings become social facts. A perceived misrepresentation of credit risk in rating implies that actors question the validity of ratings, and thus the underlying epistemic authority. This happens less because everyone knows the exact values at which ratings should be and more because intersubjective perceptions of credit riskiness deviate from rating opinions.

According to Sheng (2019), there are a number of competing explanations for China's dysfunctional rating market: regulatory arbitrage; inconsistent regulations because of the multitude of regulators; and the absence of self-regulation. Considering that, in the West, CRAs' self-regulation based on reputational self-interest did not prevent a series of rating debacles in past decades, can it really explain the flaws in the Chinese industry? As discussed in this book, a common cause of deficiencies in the global rating industry, and not just in China, relates to conflicts of interest linked to the dominant business model in the rating industry: that of "issuer pays". The issuer of a bond or security purchases the rating from the CRAs, not the investor. Being both bond issuer and client of the CRA creates the conflicts of interest in the rating industry that were a trigger in the GFC. In order to maintain old customers and acquire new ones, under the "issuer pays" business model rating analysts have an incentive to be less severe in their assessments, which comes at the cost of the quality of ratings. It is an often neglected factor in mainstream discourses on CRAs that higher competition between CRAs multiplies this effect as the customers' bargaining power increases. In the worst case, this can result in rating shopping and seriously inflated ratings.

In the Chinese case, these conflicts of interest are exacerbated. In 2009 local governments were incentivized to issue bonds to stimulate the economy. This increased the number of small CRAs (Bloomberg 2015). The promotion of small domestic CRAs has led to intensified competition on the rating market, and "issuer pays" has remained the dominant business model. A further aggravating factor that drives rating inflation in China relates to the credit rating agencies' favouring of state-owned enterprises and of bond-issuing firms that have close links to the government. These institutions enjoy implicit state guarantees that forestall default.

Rating inflation is not the only reason why the Chinese rating market is regarded as dysfunctional. The disconnect between the market's risk perception and the level of ratings is a further indicator. Interest rates "can vary by more than 3 percentage points" compared to ratings (*Financial Times* 2019b). Sheng (2019: 397) regards "the rigid redemption in China's bond market" as one of the causes of the mismatch between credit ratings and the risk premium – i.e. interest rates. Although the implicit guarantees drove ratings skyward in the past, the gradual disappearance of the rule of rigid redemption makes market sentiment more aware of the risks involved. Among various efforts to get corporate indebtedness under control, "Beijing has shown a greater willingness to let companies go insolvent to teach them a lesson about borrowing too much, and many local governments now lack the funds to help their hometown champions" (*New York Times* 2019). Since 2017 "[s]tate-backed banks were told to pull back on easy cash for state-owned enterprises and rein in risky lending. Beijing then cut much of the financial assistance that local governments had once enjoyed" (*ibid.*). The disconnect between interest rates and ratings signals that Chinese ratings are insignificant. As Kennedy (2019) puts it, "No one takes China's credit ratings seriously, least of all Chinese debt issuers and investors."

If Chinese ratings are meaningless, then why is rating inflation of concern at all? Despite the conventional view that Chinese CRAs do not matter, Chinese authorities are concerned about the systemic misrepresentation of credit risk on the rating market. As mentioned earlier, the dysfunctional domestic rating industry induced the CSRC on 17 August 2018 to impose a one-year ban on Dagong to issue new securities ratings (*South China Morning Post* 2019).[4] This rare step did not come as a surprise: in late December 2012 the NDRC had "issued tough guidelines ... that barred CRAs from soliciting customers by promising artificially inflated credit ratings, in a bid to remedy the negative impacts of the 'issuer pays' model in the credit rating business" (*China Daily* 2013). Before the ban, in March 2018, the CSRC had issued warnings to the four major Chinese CRAs (*South China Morning Post* 2019). In 2019 corporate defaults in China "surged to a record high" of $18.6 billion (*Financial Times* 2019a), whereas domestic agencies assigned high credit ratings to companies that defaulted on their bonds. At the end of 2020 CCXI – as one of the biggest Chinese rating agencies – also experienced a three-month suspension, for violating the rules set by the National Association of Financial Market Institutional Investors (NAFMII), the interbank bond market regulator (*Straits Times* 2020).

This misrepresentation of credit risk in rating is considered to have facilitated – or, at least, not prevented – a significant accumulation of debt, which enabled private companies to expand rapidly over recent years. More importantly, the regulatory actions reveal the belief that a well-functioning rating market will correct a misrepresentation of risk. Whether it was meaningless or dysfunctional in the past, the Chinese authorities want investors to rely on a well-functioning domestic rating market that is able to reflect credit risks "objectively" in order to take informed investment decisions. In other words, regardless of the state capitalist Chinese system, Chinese authorities have bet on private forms of authority to manage credit risk in order to solve the corporate debt problem.

Liberalizing China's rating market

In 2017 China committed to opening up its rating market to foreign agencies to operate branches autonomously (Bloomberg 2017). The Big Three are now allowed to run fully owned operational units on the mainland. Whether this step happened mainly as a result of the pressure exerted by the Trump administration or as a result of the dysfunctionalities of the Chinese rating market, or a combination of both factors, remains unclear. The rhetoric that accompanies the liberalization of the rating market is to discipline market participants' behaviour, to dampen risk euphoria and reduce moral hazard in the hope of restoring investor confidence and increasing rating quality. As China grapples with its own challenges on the domestic corporate bond market, according to *The Financial Times* (2018b) the "need for reliable ratings is growing". As a consequence, Fitch and S&P announced that they were to establish locally incorporated subsidiaries. In January 2018 Fitch sold its 49 per cent stake to the Singaporean sovereign wealth fund GIC (GIC 2018). Moody's is still awaiting approval by Chinese regulators for an independent credit rating licence, while it still holds 30 per cent shares in the joint venture with CCXI.

Besides dissolving previous joint ventures with local partners, the open question is how the Big Three will adapt to the Chinese context and whether their ratings may converge towards Chinese norms and characteristics. Whether the American CRAs will be able to mitigate – as they are supposed to – or end up exacerbating the problem of the misrepresentation of risk on the Chinese rating market remains to be seen. Increased competition in the rating market means higher bargaining power for rating clients because of the "issuer pays" business model. If the increase in players results in more rating inflation, then this will defeat the whole purpose of opening up the rating market. The other dilemma for the liberalization of the Chinese CRA industry is that the very companies intended to be disempowered at a global level are those whose help has been sought to help bring the domestic debt situation under control, changing the dynamic of the Chinese ambition for global rating hegemony.

It is premature to declare China's attempts to challenge the American rating oligopoly a failure. Whether China can live up to its expectations of transforming the global rating landscape remains uncertain, at least in the medium term. The rating debacle of the American Big Three in the course of the 2008 global financial crisis offered a special opportunity to the Chinese challenger to go global and portray itself as the promising reformer of an obviously deficient governance of the global financial system. This window of opportunity may have opened too early, however. China's corporate debt problems and the mismanagement of credit risk manifested by rating inflation have hampered China's efforts for now. Although the challenger had been temporarily banned from operations for bad business practices and taken over by a government institution, those supposedly challenged, the American Big Three, are now considered knights in shining armour.

In order to make sense of this intricate situation, the wider context needs to be considered. The development of the Chinese bond market to be the second largest in the world, alongside its emulation of the American credit rating system, including its flaws, seemingly signals China's willingness to pursue the path of Western-style financial globalization. It also signals acceptance of the fragmentation of authority that comes with a more market-oriented financial system and a certain willingness by Chinese regulators to cooperate, rather than to compete, for an alternative rating system. There is a central caveat in the Chinese context, however. In the United States, the Big Three are protected from liability claims by the First Amendment of the US Constitution. Their credit ratings are regarded as opinions in legal terms regardless of their authoritative status. Given the politically salient aspect of freedom of speech in China, it is questionable how far China's leadership will go in facilitating a functioning credit rating system. This dilemma points to a larger question regarding the fundamental incompatibility of pursuing financial liberalism without political liberalism. The developments in credit rating, particularly the impact of international CRAs operating in the Chinese market, offer an experiment in this regard.

Apart from that, it is questionable whether a global rating system under Chinese rule will be more stable and less prone to crisis than it is today. The CRA regulations enacted after the global financial crisis, as discussed in Chapter 5, demonstrate just how difficult it is to bring effective and meaningful reforms – whether it concerns, for example, the analytics of ratings, the "issuer pays" business model or the undoing of hard-wired ratings in financial regulation.

Indeed, China's willingness to pursue the path of Western-style financialization and financial disintermediation is an open question in scholarly circles. Depending on how we answer this question, we can develop two scenarios for the future of rating. If we assume that China plays the role of the system "taker", then it is likely that in the medium term the existing, authoritative CRAs will continue to play a constitutive role in global finance and provide a critical piece of its infrastructure. In the long run, I would also not exclude a Chinese company embracing the existing norms and succeeding in joining the global rating oligopoly. In other words, wherever their headquarters are located, the CRAs' influence is unlikely to decrease in the future for this scenario.

If, instead, China is able to shape the global financial system according to its own terms, then rating may fulfil a different function and be the diffuser of different norms. We may observe a change in the dominant understanding of creditworthiness on global financial markets. For example, sovereigns that borrow on international bond markets will have to adapt to "Chinese" norms and ideas of economic, fiscal and monetary policy – whatever definition this entails – in order to have access to capital. It is difficult to predict which of these two scenarios will prevail. Reality will probably fall somewhere in between. Given the complexities and contingencies of the future, it is fair to say that the modification of the existing global rating order and its normative evolution will happen only on a piecemeal basis rather than in a disruptive fashion.

CONCLUSION

This book aims to enhance the understanding of credit rating agencies as constitutive actors in global financial capitalism. The relevance of these institutions goes far beyond the seemingly technical world of finance. A deeper understanding of the pervasiveness of credit ratings in today's financial markets raises awareness of the industry's political and social importance. It is not only corporations, banks and governments that are subject to the consequential judgements of these private companies. Academic institutions, infrastructure and transportation entities such as port authorities, highway operators and other public good providers in the health and medical sector are rated, as soon as they aspire to have access to international capital markets to refinance themselves.

The purpose of this book is not to criticize the CRAs for the sake of criticism. If this were the case, it would just contribute a further (probably unnecessary) line of argument to the already existing and extensive CRA critique. This book is an attempt to go beyond the conventional functionalist reading of the credit rating agencies' role, which basically reduces the CRAs to institutions that decrease information asymmetries on financial markets. Ironically, the public attention paid to the CRAs in the course of the GFC has contributed to the corroboration of such preconceived notions about CRAs among policy-makers, practitioners, the media and scholars.

The agencies' work is not replicable, and the oligopoly not easily replaced. CRAs do not discover ratings, as if the information about credit risk pre-exists, free from interpretation; they create ratings. Ratings are social constructions that rest on certain interpretations of the material world. Therefore, it is important to acknowledge the contingent character of assessing creditworthiness. In their capacity of epistemic authority, CRAs define the relevant knowledge about credit risk assessment. This allows them to exert narrative authority in the discourse about creditworthiness. In order to make disintermediated markets work, an epistemic authority that issues centralized judgements on creditworthiness is inevitable. A functionalist reading misses exactly this authoritative dimension of the agencies' work, while underestimating the systematic role of the agencies: CRAs do not only decrease information asymmetries but, most importantly, coordinate market expectations, fix meanings and establish commonly held interpretations of debt issuers' creditworthiness.

With such a conceptualization of rating in mind, the idea of "rating failure" needs to be revaluated. From the point of view that posits ratings as social constructions, the notion that ratings misrepresent credit risk is problematic, as it implies that ratings deviate from an imagined true, correct and objective level.[1] There is, however, no exogenous and given rating to be discovered by the CRAs in the first place, if only they did their job properly. If investors acknowledge the commonly shared, intersubjective interpretation of creditworthiness diffused by the authoritative agencies, ratings become social facts. A perceived misrepresentation of credit risk in rating implies that actors question the validity of ratings, and thus the CRAs' underlying epistemic authority. This happens not so much because everyone knows the exact values at which ratings should be, but because intersubjective perceptions of credit risk start to deviate from the rating opinions of authoritative agencies. As in the lead-up to the global financial crisis of 2008, once investors had lost confidence and moved into a stage of radical uncertainty, the rating bubble burst and dramatic financial losses ensued.

This book offers a critical engagement with the CRAs and their work, revealing the blind spots in the CRA debate and advancing the state of knowledge about the specificity of the CRAs' authority in global financial capitalism. Considering the experience of the GFC and the CRAs' immunity to it, the puzzle of the CRAs' authority has proved to be even more compelling. To avoid misunderstandings, the critical lens has not entailed a questioning of the CRAs' expertise or work ethic. The assumption that rating analysts and officials "are thoughtful and focused individuals with an excellent grasp of the wider economic world" (Sinclair 1999: 164) neither implies the impossibility of a critical inquiry into the CRAs' epistemic authority nor renders this inquiry automatically apologetic.

Credit ratings are emblematic of the bigger phenomenon of "financialization", which started with the end of the Bretton Woods system in the 1970s (see, for example, Krippner 2011). New players in the shape of rising powers are now entering the governance of the global economy, which poses even more questions about the future of global finance and, thus, credit rating. To what extent, for example, will the BRICS countries (Brazil, Russia, India, China and South Africa) influence the shape of global financial capitalism (Henning & Walter 2016)? What will happen to the older powers in the new constellation of global finance? The answers are not yet obvious. For the CRAs, it is still uncertain whether players that are emerging in other parts of the world will succeed in challenging the persistent US oligopoly.

Nevertheless, the rating market is becoming not just more competitive and global but also more heterogeneous, not least in terms of rating opinions. If rating agencies are regarded as representatives of investors' interests (Ouroussoff 2010) and given that investors' national and cultural backgrounds are changing, different understandings of creditworthiness may prevail. Against this backdrop, will the Big Three remain the world's predominant epistemic authority in terms of creditworthiness, or will we experience a power shift? How will different worldviews and normative assumptions translate into rating practices? China is at the front in taking the Big Three on. Nevertheless, challenging the status quo does not happen by replacing the Big Three but, rather, by inviting them in. What the impact of the Big Three's presence in China will be, and how the Big Three will change themselves through their operations in China, remain to be seen.

Another context in which the CRAs will play a pivotal role given their authority concerns climate change and the ecological crisis. When it comes to greening the financial system or the transition to a low-carbon economy, CRAs have the ability to enable change, but they can also act as a force for the status quo. They can make it costlier or more affordable for companies and states to undertake the necessary investments and measures to fight climate change. They can punish or support companies and states to adapt to and mitigate climate change risks. It will require further research to analyse how CRAs position themselves in this context, and what the role of environmental, social and governance (ESG) ratings and corporate sustainability assessments will be in relation to the CRAs' "usual" business. Will the latter disappear completely at some point?

Likewise, the future of rating will also be subject to developments in the area of artificial intelligence (AI) and fintech. Algorithms that can process "big data" may deliver the basis on which CRAs will take rating actions. The application of algorithms for ratings of individuals is already a common practice. There is awareness about the pro-cyclical or performative effects of these technologies, which can even increase biases instead of correcting them. Important though it is to keep track of how the CRAs come to their decision-making, the use of sophisticated technology will not solve the issue that rating will remain judgement about creditworthiness, which is performative in itself if the judgement is expressed by a few authoritative institutions that are followed by most market participants.

Furthermore, it is important not only how the agencies react to developments in the financial industry but also how the agencies assess them. Whether it be digital currencies, cryptocurrencies, algorithmic trading or the pre-eminence of passive investment tools and its consequence for companies' ownership and leadership, to name just a few, how do the agencies rate the creditworthiness of the institutions affected by these developments? Will institutions become financially more healthy or risky? At the same time, these developments raise questions about the safety and the stability of the financial system as a whole. To be fair, considerations regarding systemic risk obviously transcend the job of the agencies. It is questionable whether CRAs are equipped with the appropriate mandate to be the watchdog of financial markets and raise the red flag if necessary in the light of the manifold changes that are happening simultaneously. In the end, the GFC demonstrated how detrimental it can be if only the financial health of individual institutions is on the regulatory radar. Even if Basel III is trying to correct the micro-prudential regulatory approach with a more macro-prudential agenda, we should not forget that regulatory reliance on CRA ratings continues. This implies, first, that the micro-prudential regulation of credit risk is still active and, second, that the CRAs' views on the abovementioned new developments matter, and their assessments of the related credit risks are consequential.

Before I conclude, a few words are in order on the role of the media and its relationship to the CRAs' authority. In order to fully grasp the CRAs' role in the discursive construction of creditworthiness, further research is required to systematically examine the media coverage of rating events. The CRAs' epistemic authority is reproduced with references such as "CRAs praise successful crisis management" (Spiegel 2013, own translation), or citing explicit warnings such as "Fitch warned it could downgrade Italy's sovereign rating further if the recession ran deeper and longer than expected" (*New York Times* 2013). Furthermore, how the media frames rating actions matters as well. Catchy headlines and a rhetoric of "carrot and stick" not only shapes the perception of debt issuers' creditworthiness but also defines the relevant cause-and-effect chains. For example, referring to "highly indebted Cyprus" favours the narrative of a prodigal fiscal policy rather than a bankrupt financial sector. When the global financial crisis was redefined into a sovereign debt crisis in Europe, rating events facilitated a redefinition of prodigal fiscal policy as the cause of the crisis, taking the place of the expensive rescue of the financial sector. By defining the symptoms for the cause, not only do the mechanisms that had led to a certain situation disappear into oblivion, but narratives that legitimize this obliviousness are also (re-)activated. This is done most easily with problems that may already have existed in the past, such as "structural problems" in certain countries of the euro area. This story could not have been told without a specific type of media coverage about rating events.

Moreover, the extent to which the media, press agencies and relevant financial market information providers (e.g. Bloomberg, Thomson Reuters, *The Financial Times*, *The Wall Street Journal*, *The Economist*, etc.) exert structural power on CRAs also deserves closer scrutiny. This aspect becomes even more compelling if we consider that publishing houses and media concerns are showing an increased interest in the rating business, as the Hearst Corporation in the case of Fitch demonstrates. Whether this will contribute to more "independence and credibility" of rating remains to be seen (Engelen 2004: 65). The nexus and interactions between the different cells of the network of epistemic authorities on financial markets, of which the CRAs are one, shapes how meaning is produced in global financial capitalism more than commonly acknowledged.

As policy-makers stick to conventional understandings of ratings that equate rating with a technical and apolitical exercise, they can circumvent uncomfortable questions about authority and responsibility. If we accept that financial markets cannot work without the CRAs' judgements, which means that the CRAs' authority is inevitable, then it is up to politics to give an answer to the resulting accountability gap given that the CRAs cannot be held liable. We cannot expect the agencies to do that, as it is simply not their job. If governments do not want to undertake the creditworthiness assessment themselves, the delegation of authority for the public's exposure to credit risk has to be accompanied with liability. It is just too easy to deflect the responsibility to the CRAs when things go wrong but enjoy when someone else is "making the sorts of judgements otherwise (and previously) reserved for government regulators" (Abdelal 2007: 171) in good times. To close the accountability gap is surely not an easy undertaking, as the different attempts of regulating the CRA industry have shown. If the answer is to disempower the agencies, then more capabilities have to mobilized to find alternatives to CRA ratings. The fact that there is currently no alternative to CRA ratings is attributable to a path dependence, which is the cause and result of the CRAs' authority. To break this path dependence amounts to a paradigm shift, and will imply working against market conventions and habit. In the end, it is often the market participants themselves who do not wish to abolish CRA ratings.

When the next financial crisis hits, no doubt the agencies' authority will be closely scrutinized again. The GFC has shown, however, that the agitation regarding the CRAs has not really materialized as a serious rethinking of the CRAs' role in financial markets. Once the political pressure after a crisis has faded, the law of inertia prevails, and the desire to return to normal pushes lessons learned from the crisis into the background.

NOTES

Introduction

1. In financial jargon, bonds belong to the category of "fixed-income" products.
2. Investors can be also referred to as lenders, while debt issuers are borrowers.
3. "Financialized capitalism" refers to the pervasive role of financial markets, including its motives, actors and institutions, in the operation of the global economy (Epstein 2005: 3). The process of financialization propels the dominance of the financial sector over the real, productive economy (Krippner 2011; Nölke & Perry 2007), implying the transnationalization of control and power structures – the diffusion and decentralization of authority (Strange 1998).
4. In April 2010 Standard & Poor's downgraded Greece to BB+, Portugal to A− and Spain to AA within two days. One month later Fitch downgraded Spain to AA+. For a timeline of key sovereign debt events, see BIS (2011: 46, Annex 3).
5. According to Katz and Shapiro (1985: 424), a network externality exists when the "utility that a user derives from consumption of the good increases with the number of other agents consuming the good".
6. Since the US financial markets represent the epicentre of today's global financial system, with the dominant role of the US dollar as the world's leading currency, this is not surprising.
7. "Securitization" refers to securitized assets. Such securities often contain assets of different credit risk quality. Ratings facilitate that credit risk is tradeable by providing a base on which to price it.
8. "Maturity transformation" refers to the refinancing of long-term assets with short-term liabilities. It is a typical challenge that classical financial intermediaries, such as banks, face.
9. Admittedly, in positivist jargon, in which the assumption is that information is consumed as it is without interpretive frames that are intersubjectively shared, more ratings would lead to an increase in "cognitive" information asymmetry.
10. That is, asset-backed securities and collateralized debt obligations, respectively.
11. The GFC itself can be read as a "run on the shadow banking system", which started in 2007 with the questioning of securitized collateral (Tarullo 2013; Blyth 2013; Pozsar *et al.* 2010; Mehrling 2010).
12. The division between investment grade and non-investment grade is based on the structure of the rating scale, the former referring to securities rated in the upper half of the rating scale, the latter to those rated in the lower half. For more details, see Chapter 2.
13. Prior to the acquisition by Morningstar Inc. in 2019, the name of the predecessor institution was Dominion Bond Rating Service (DBRS).

1 The "what" and the "who" about credit rating

1. See "Intro to credit ratings", at www.spglobal.com/ratings/en/about/intro-to-credit-ratings.
2. In older documents published by CRAs, ratings may still be classified as probabilities of default. With increased public scrutiny, CRAs have become more cautious in their external communications as to what they claim.
3. "Positivism" in the social sciences refers to the idea that social reality is not socially constructed but is taken as given and exists independently from interpretation. It implies that we can objectively measure this reality, and that there is no interaction between the subject and the object of measurement. Further, conceiving markets as social and political constructs contrasts the positivist understanding of markets as ahistorical, mechanistic creatures that exhibit law-like forms of behaviour (Krippner 2011).
4. According to McCloskey (1983: 487), "predictionism" is a symptom of scientism or modernism. Drawing on Mises (1949: 867), McCloskey notes that prediction of the economic future is "beyond the power of any mortal man", and thus "impossible for economics", not to mention for CRAs.
5. I want to thank Mark Blyth for this expression, which hits the nail on the head.
6. "Market-based finance" is associated with financial disintermediation, sometimes also called the marketization of banking, and phenomena such as securitization, helping credit risks to be able to travel. These concepts are elaborated further below.
7. See "Intro to credit ratings", at www.spglobal.com/ratings/en/about/intro-to-credit-ratings.
8. The commodification of rating implies further conflicts of interest, which are, of course, not denied in a functionalist perspective. For example, the dominant rating business model, "issuer pays", has gained prominence in the course of the global financial crisis as a result of the distorted incentive for CRAs to rate their clients (i.e. debt issuers) more leniently.
9. See "The free dictionary", at www.thefreedictionary.com/creditworthy.
10. See https://money.cnn.com/quote/shareholders/shareholders.html?symb=SPGI&sub View=institutional.
11. To learn more about "American asset manager capitalism", corporate power and the "new political economy of corporate governance", see Braun (2021).
12. See "About S&P Global ratings", at www.spglobal.com/ratings/en/about.
13. Standard & Poor's (2017a: 18).
14. *Ibid.*: 31.
15. *Ibid.,* 34.
16. *Ibid.*, 28.
17. *Ibid.*, 32.
18. *Ibid.*, 34.
19. See "About S&P Global Ratings", at www.spglobal.com/ratings/en/about.
20. *Ibid.*
21. For an insightful biography on Henry Varnum Poor, see Chandler (1956).
22. See "A history of Standard and Poor's, beginnings, 1830–69", at www.standardandpoors.com/about-sp/timeline/en/us.
23. No trace of an exact founding date has been found for "Poor's Railroad Manual Company".
24. For a detailed account of the intertwined origins of Moody's and Standard and Poor's, see Sinclair (2005: 25, fig. 1).
25. "A history of Standard and Poor's, beginnings, 1915–40", at www.standardandpoors.com/about-sp/timeline/en/us.
26. See https://money.cnn.com/quote/shareholders/shareholders.html?symb=MCO&sub View=institutional.
27. Moody's Investors Service (2017: 31).
28. *Ibid.*: 37.

29. *Ibid.*, 42.
30. *Ibid.*, 44.
31. *Ibid.*, 16, 40, 51.
32. *Ibid.*, 11.
33. "Moody's history: a century of market leadership", at www.moodys.com/Pages/atc001. aspx. In addition to the credit reporting agencies, the specialized financial press and investment bankers are also considered to be institutional predecessors of the CRAs (Sylla 2002).
34. *Ibid.*
35. One example of a mercantile credit reporting firm at the time was R. G. Dun & Company. In 1962 the successor institution, the Dun & Bradstreet Corporation, then a business information provider, purchased Moody's Investors Service. Since 1998 Moody's has been the bond credit rating subsidiary of NYSE-listed Moody's Corporation (Sinclair 2005: 25).
36. "Moody's history: a century of market leadership", at www.moodys.com/Pages/atc001. aspx.
37. See www.fitchratings.com and www.hearst.com/fitch-group.
38. Abbreviated as BMI, providing financial information, country risk and industry analysis specializing in emerging and frontier markets.
39. *Ibid.*, 8, 88.
40. See Fimalac (2004).
41. Information taken at the time from the web page www.fimalac.com/History-of-the-group-1992-2005.html; although the link no longer works, the author can verify the information on request.
42. *Ibid.*
43. For more details about the different pricing policies of rating agencies in general, see Mattarocci (2014: 67–80).
44. For example, Moody's regularly publishes a list of unsolicited ratings, which includes corporate and public entities.
45. This is not to say that there is no cooperation at all between sovereigns and the CRAs in the case of unsolicited sovereign ratings. A high-ranking CRA representative in charge of sovereign ratings described the relationship as an "interactive process" between the CRA and the respective governments (Hinrichs 2012).
46. Chapter 2 discusses the concept of sovereign ceiling.

2 What do credit rating agencies do?

1. See the *Oxford English Dictionary*, for example.
2. Examples of supranational debt issuers are, for example, multilateral development banks, such as the Inter-American Development Bank (IDB) and the International Investment Bank (IIB).
3. The Basel III Accord is an international regulatory regime set up to regulate the minimum capital requirements for banks, among others. Within the "standardized approach" of the Basel III Accord, risk categories are constituted by external CRA ratings. For an informative and critical discussion of Basel II and its successor, Basel III, see Lall (2012).
4. "About S&P Global Ratings", at www.spglobal.com/ratings/en/about.
5. "Long-term" refers to the fact that the original maturity of bonds or obligations is a minimum of one year, usually more.
6. How it can be feasible that all countries in the eurozone become net exporters while trading with each other is another story (Blyth 2013).
7. "Intro to Credit Ratings", at www.spglobal.com/ratings/en/about/intro-to-credit-ratings.
8. *Ibid.*

9. "Mid-range ratings" refer to ratings without "+" or "−" modifiers and to the ratings with suffix "2" for Moody's.

10. In Moody's terms, "Baa" is classified as the last investment-grade category. The appended numerical modifier "3" indicates a ranking at the lower end of that rating category. The company notes that "obligations rated Baa are judged to be medium-grade and subject to moderate credit risk and as such may possess certain speculative characteristics" (Moody's Investors Service 2013b: 5).

11. See www.spglobal.com/ratings/en/about/understanding-ratings.

12. In earlier published sovereign rating methodologies, S&P referred to these assessments explicitly as "scores"; for example, see Standard & Poor's (2012a: 3).

13. In earlier published sovereign rating methodologies, S&P referred to the institutional assessment as the "political score"; for example, see Standard & Poor's (2012a: 3).

14. The 2017 version of the published S&P sovereign rating methodology does not contain any reference to the rating committee even though it acknowledges its existence in the general description of the rating process on its website; see www.spglobal.com/ratings/en/about/understanding-ratings.

15. This statement was made in the context of an academic conference during a panel discussion in November 2012.

16. In the case of Moody's, a synonym for being on review is when an issuer is "on watch", or on the "Watchlist" (Moody's Investors Service 2020a: 30).

17. The use of third-party indicators as rating input is a case of "interdiscursivity". The reproduction of indicators from international organizations and other renowned institutions facilitates the recontextualization and diffusion of certain narratives across discourses, synchronically and diachronically.

3 The use of ratings

1. "Who uses credit ratings?", at www.spglobal.com/ratings/en/about/understanding-ratings.

2. *Ibid.*

3. *Ibid.*

4. See the ECB website: www.ecb.europa.eu/paym/coll/risk/ecaf/html/index.en.html.

5. See the ECB website: www.ecb.europa.eu/paym/coll/standards/nonmarketable/html/index.en.html.

6. See the ECB website: www.ecb.europa.eu/paym/coll/standards/marketable/html/index.en.html.

7. The accepted external credit assessment institutions in the Eurosystem credit assessment framework comprise the Big Three and the largest Canadian credit rating agency, DBRS Morningstar. Table 2.1 refers to long-term ratings, the relevant rating type for sovereign ratings and other marketable assets in collateral ECB frameworks.

8. The extent to which the CRAs are willing to bear the regulatory intrusion into their business operations in exchange for their privileged status as ECAIs in the ECB's collateral framework is another story.

9. See the April and October issues of the ECB *Monthly Bulletin*. The ECB repealed these measures in March 2013; see the May 2013 *Monthly Bulletin*.

10. In Fitch's terminology, rating outlooks "indicate the direction a rating is likely to move over a one- to two-year period". Watches, instead, are "typically event-driven". They are "generally resolved over a relatively short period" of about six months (Fitch 2020: 7–8).

11. Given that the ratings of the Big Three are strongly correlated, procyclicality is even exacerbated. For empirical evidence, see, for example, Gaillard (2012).

12. For an informative and critical discussion of Basel II and its successor, Basel III, see Lall (2012).

13. See sections 939–939A in US Congress (2010).
14. Chapter 5 focuses on the regulation of CRAs, including the IOSCO "Code of conduct fundamentals for credit rating agencies".
15. SEC web page www.sec.gov/spotlight/dodd-frank.shtml; this provides information on the status of the adoption of the Dodd–Frank provisions.
16. For an overview of the financial reforms after the global financial crisis and a discussion about the continued delegation of "discretion to private actors", see Porter (2014).

4 Credit rating agencies under criticism

1. For the same reason, there are warnings against introducing solicited sovereign ratings. In such a scenario, sovereign ratings could suffer from a positive bias, as sovereigns would become the CRAs' clients.
2. This is to differentiate from the CRAs' US home bias.

5 Regulating the credit rating agencies

1. See Moody's Investors Service (2001) and Bloomberg (2001) for the rating actions on 28 November 2001. For a concise account of the Enron debacle, including the CRAs' role in it, see Sinclair (2005: 167–72), Partnoy (2003: 296–349) and Coffee (2006: 34–5).
2. See section 702(b) of the Sarbanes–Oxley Act.
3. For a summary, see SEC (2003b: 10–15).
4. The Credit Rating Agency Reform Act consists in the amendment of the Securities Exchange Act of 1934 by section 15E, "Registration of Nationally Recognized Statistical Rating Organizations".
5. See section 2 of the Credit Rating Agency Reform Act (US Congress 2006).
6. See the SEC web page www.sec.gov/ocr/ocr-current-nrsros.html.
7. See section 932, on the "Enhanced Regulation, Accountability, and Transparency of Nationally Recognized Statistical Rating Organizations", title IX, subsection C (US Congress 2010).
8. See the OCR website: www.sec.gov/ocr.
9. The SEC's final rules make amendments and add new subsections to rules 17g and 15-Ga under the Securities Exchange Act of 1934.
10. The 1982 amendment to Section 11 of the 1933 Securities Act constitutes SEC Rule 436(g), providing the legal foundation for the exemption regime; see also Gaillard and Harrington (2016: 40). The effort to repeal Rule 436(g) has proved to be a futile undertaking.
11. Ordinary members of IOSCO are national securities commissions or similar governmental bodies with significant authority over securities or derivatives markets. There are also associate and affiliate members in IOSCO, the latter including non-state actors. For more details, see the IOSCO website: www.iosco.org/about/?subsection=becoming_a_member.
12. In 2011 the Committee of European Securities Regulators was superseded by the European Securities and Markets Authority, which is part of the European System of Financial Supervision.
13. The Capital Requirements Directive consists of Directive 2006/48/EC (European Parliament, Council of the European Union 2006a) and Directive 2006/49/EC (European Parliament, Council of the European Union 2006b). Because of the implementation of Basel III in 2013, it has been replaced by Directive 2013/36/EU (European Parliament, Council of the European Union 2013b).

14. The Economic and Financial Affairs Council consists of the economics and finance ministers from all EU member states. It is in charge of EU policy in three main areas: economic policy, taxation and the regulation of financial services. Relevant European commissioners also participate in the ECOFIN meetings. For more details, see: www.consilium.europa. eu/en/council-eu/configurations/ecofin.
15. Regulation (EC) 1060/2009 entered into force in December 2009. As a result of the creation of ESMA, the regulation was amended in May 2011.
16. The regulatory package of 21 May 2013 consists of Regulation (EU) 462/2013 (European Parliament, Council of the European Union 2013c) and Directive 2013/14/EU (European Parliament, Council of the European Union 2013a).
17. This is not to say that competition or transparency are not good things per se.
18. The following sections of this chapter draw upon Mennillo and Sinclair (2019).

6 Credit rating in China

1. See website of Dagong Hong Kong, "About us".
2. S&P's downgrade to AA– had occurred two years beforehand in the course of the previous debt ceiling debates (Reuters 2011b).
3. An alternative way to refer to ratings' misrepresentation of credit risk is "rating failure".
4. Despite the ban, Dagong branches outside China continued to operate and to issue sovereign ratings.

Conclusion

1. Misrepresentation of credit risk can refer both to an underestimation of credit risk (namely to excessively favourable judgements) and to an overestimation of credit risk (namely to excessively unfavourable judgements).

REFERENCES

Abdelal, R. 2007. *Capital Rules: The Construction of Global Finance*. Cambridge, MA: Harvard University Press.

Abdelal, R. 2009. "Constructivism as an approach to international political economy". In *Routledge Handbook of International Political Economy (IPE): IPE as a Global Conversation*, M. Blyth (ed.), 62–76. Abingdon: Routledge.

Abdelal, R. & M. Blyth 2015. "Just who put you in charge? We did: credit rating agencies and the politics of ratings". In *Ranking the World: Grading States as a Tool of Global Governance*, A. Cooley & J. Snyder (eds), 39–59. Cambridge: Cambridge University Press.

Afonso, A., D. Furceri & P. Gomes 2012. "Sovereign credit ratings and financial markets linkages: application to European data". *Journal of International Money and Finance* 31 (3): 606–38.

Alden, W. 2014. "Hearst to buy control of Fitch, the credit ratings firm". *New York Times*, 12 December. Available at: http://dealbook.nytimes.com/2014/12/12/hearst-to-buy-cont rol-of-credit-ratings-firm-fitch/?r=0.

Amtenbrink, F. & J. de Haan 2009. "Regulating credit ratings in the European Union: a critical first assessment of Regulation 1060/2009 on credit rating agencies". *Common Market Law Review* 46 (6): 1915–49.

Amtenbrink, F. & K. Heine 2013. "Regulating credit rating agencies in the European Union: lessons from behavioural science". *Dovenschmidt Quarterly* 2 (1): 2–15.

Barducci, M. & T. Fest 2011. "Evaluation of the regulations of credit rating agencies in the United States and the European Community". Available at: http://papers.ssrn.com/sol3/papers.cfm?abstractid=1803132.

Bartels, B. & B. Weder di Mauro 2013. "A rating agency for Europe: a good idea?". VoxEu, 4 July. Available at: www.voxeu.org/article/rating-agency-europe-good-idea.

BBC News 2013. "Italy's credit rating has been downgraded by S&P". 9 July. Available at: www.bbc.com/news/business-23250689.

BCBS 2009. *Strengthening the Resilience of the Banking Sector: Consultative Document*. Basel: BCBS.

BCBS 2014. *Revisions to the Standardised Approach for Credit Risk: Consultative Document*. Basel: BCBS.

BCBS 2015. *Revisions to the Standardised Approach for Credit Risk: Second Consultative Document*. Basel: BCBS.

BCBS 2017. "High-level summary of Basel III reforms". Basel: BCBS.

Besedovsky, N. 2012. "Politischer Ritterschlag für Ratingagenturen: Regulatorisches Outsourcing und der Beitrag von Gesetzgebern zur Macht der Ratingagenturen". In *Entfesselte Finanzmärkte: Soziologische Analysen des Modernen Kapitalismus*, K. Kraemer & S. Nessel (eds), 225–42. Frankfurt: Campus Verlag.

Bhatia, A. 2002. "Sovereign credit ratings methodology: an evaluation", Working Paper WP/02/170. Washington, DC: IMF.

BIS 2011. "The impact of sovereign credit risk on bank funding conditions", Committee on the Global Financial System Paper 43. Basel: BIS.

Blodget, H. 2011. "Moody's Analyst Breaks Silence: Says Ratings Agency Rotten To Core With Conflicts". Business Insider, 19 August. Available at: www.businessinsider.com/moodys-analyst-conflicts-corruption-and-greed-2011-8?r=US&IR=T.

Bloomberg 2001. "S&P cuts Enron credit rating to junk status". 28 November. Available at: www.bloomberg.com/news/articles/2001-11-27/s-and-p-cuts-enron-credit-rating-to-junk-status.

Bloomberg 2011. "Ireland's rating cut to BBB+ by S&P as bank rescue costs hit $142 billion". 1 April. Available at: www.bloomberg.com/news/articles/2011-04-01/ireland-s-debt-rating-is-reduced-one-level-to-bbb-by-s-p-on-banking-costs.

Bloomberg 2015. "China rating companies say honesty doesn't pay as risks ignored". 1 April. Available at: www.bloomberg.com/news/articles/2015-03-31/china-rating-companies-say-honesty-doesn-t-pay-as-risks-ignored.

Bloomberg 2017. "China's bond-exchange giant shows domestic ratings too high". 25 October. Available at: www.bloomberg.com/news/articles/2017-10-24/chinas-bond-exchange-giant-shows-domestic-ratings-are-too-high.

Bloomberg 2020. "Fed Unbound: All the U.S. Central Bank's Corona-Related Moves". 26 March. Available at: www.bloomberg.com/news/articles/2020-03-25/fed-unbound-all-the-u-s-central-bank-s-corona-related-moves.

Blyth, M. 2013. *Austerity: The History of a Dangerous Idea*. Oxford: Oxford University Press.

Boot, A., T. Milbourn & A. Schmeits 2006. "Credit ratings as coordination mechanisms". *Review of Financial Studies* 19 (1): 81–118.

Braun, B. 2021. "Asset manager capitalism as a corporate governance regime". In *The American Political Economy: Politics, Markets, and Power*, J. Hacker *et al.* (eds), 270–94. Cambridge: Cambridge University Press.

Brooks, R., R. Faff, D. Hillier & J. Hillier 2004. "The national market impact of sovereign rating changes". *Journal of Banking & Finance* 28 (1): 233–50.

Bruce, R. 1992. "Debt-rating agencies fill the gap". *New York Times*, 14 November. Available at: www.nytimes.com/1992/11/14/your-money/14iht-mrca.html.

Brummer, C. & R. Loko 2014. "The new politics of transatlantic credit rating agency regulation". In *Transnational Financial Regulation after the Crisis*, T. Porter (ed.), 154–76. Abingdon: Routledge.

Bruner, C. & R. Abdelal 2005. "To judge Leviathan: sovereign credit ratings, national law, and the world economy". *Journal of Public Policy* 25 (2): 191–217.

Brunnermeier, M. *et al.* 2009. "The fundamental principles of financial regulation", Geneva Reports on the World Economy 11. Geneva: International Center for Monetary and Banking Studies.

Buhse, M. 2014. "Das Monopol der Schwarzseher". *Die Zeit*, 30 January.

Cantor, R. & F. Packer 1996. "Determinants and impact of sovereign credit ratings". *Economic Policy Review* 2 (2): 37–54.

Carruthers, B. 2013. "From uncertainty toward risk: the case of credit ratings". *Socio-Economic Review* 11 (3): 525–51.

CEBS 2006. "Guidelines on the recognition of external credit assessment institutions". London: CEBS.

CESR 2005. "CESR's technical advice to the European Commission on possible measures concerning credit rating agencies", CESR/05~139b. Paris: CESR.

CESR 2008a. "CESR's second report to the European Commission on the compliance of credit rating agencies with the IOSCO Code and the role of credit rating agencies in structured finance", CESR/08~277. Paris: CESR.

CESR 2008b. "Role of credit rating agencies: ESME's report to the European Commission". Paris: CESR.

Chandler, Jr, A. 1956. *Henry Varnum Poor: Business Editor, Analyst, and Reformer*. Cambridge, MA: Harvard University Press.

Chen, A. & O. Everling 2002. "Finanzsystem und rating in China". *Die Bank* 11: 727–31.

China Daily 2013. "The Chinese credit rating industry". 26 July. Available at: www.chinadailyasia. com/focus-hk/article-409.html.

CNN Money 2011. "Dow plunges after S&P downgrade". 8 August. Available at: http://money. cnn.com/2011/08/08/markets/marketsnewyork/index.htm.

Coffee, Jr, J. 2006. *Gatekeepers: The Professions and Corporate Governance*. Oxford: Oxford University Press.

Coffee, Jr, J. 2011. "Ratings reform: the good, the bad, and the ugly". *Harvard Business Law Review* 1: 231–78.

Council of the European Union 2007a. "Council conclusions on enhancing the arrangements for financial stability in the EU: 2822nd Economic and Financial Affairs Council meeting". Luxembourg: Council of the European Union.

Council of the European Union 2007b. "Press release: 2822nd Council meeting, Economic and Financial Affairs", Press Release 13571/07 (Presse 217). 9 October.

Council of the European Union 2008. "Press release: 2894th Council meeting, Economic and Financial Affairs", Press Release 13784/08 (Presse 279). 7 October.

Council on Foreign Relations 2015. "The credit rating controversy". 19 February. Available at: www.cfr.org/backgrounder/credit-rating-controversy.

Cousin, V. 2007. *Banking in China*. Basingstoke: Palgrave Macmillan.

Dagong Europe 2016. "Dagong Europe company profile", press release. 20 July.

Dagong Global Credit Rating 2015. "大公主权信用评级方法" ["Dagong's sovereign credit method"]. Beijing: Dagong Global Credit Rating.

Dagong Global Credit Rating n.d. "Reform the international rating system to promote the world economic recovery".

Dagong Hong Kong 2015. "Dagong sovereign credit rating methodology". Hong Kong: Dagong Global Credit Rating (Hong Kong).

De Haan, J. & F. Amtenbrink 2011. "Credit rating agencies", Working Paper 278. Amsterdam: De Nederlandsche Bank.

Dullien, S. 2013. "Financial market reform: still too much faith in market rationality". *Wirtschaftsdienst* 93 (1), supplement: 23–9.

ECB 2013. *Collateral Eligibility Requirements: A Comparative Study across Specific Frameworks*. Frankfurt: ECB.

ECB 2014. "Eurosystem credit assessment framework for monetary policy operations" [box 3]. *Monthly Bulletin*, April: 28–31.

ECB 2015. "ECB announces expanded asset purchase programme", press release. 22 January. Available at: www.ecb.europa.eu/press/pr/date/2015/html/pr150122_1.en.html.

Eijffinger, S. 2012. "Rating agencies: role and influence of their sovereign credit risk assessment in the eurozone". *Journal of Common Market Studies* 50 (6): 912–21.

Engelen, K. 2004. "Das Empire strikes back". *The International Economy* 18 (1): 64–71.

Epstein, G. 2005. *Financialization and the World Economy*. Cheltenham: Edward Elgar.

ESMA 2015. "Call for evidence: competition, choice and conflicts of interest in the credit rating industry", ESMA/2015/233. Paris: ESMA.

ESMA 2021. "Report on CRA Market Share calculation", ESMA80-416-197. Paris: ESMA.

EUobserver 2012. "Merkel: 'loves' Europe, insists on 'homework'". 18 December. Available at: https://euobserver.com/economic/118555.

European Commission 2006. "Communication from the Commission on credit rating agencies (2006/C 59/02)". *Official Journal of the European Union*, 11 March, C 59/2–6.

European Commission 2008a. "Commission communication on financial stability: frequently asked questions", Press Release MEMO/08/123. 27 February.

European Commission 2008b. "Proposal for a Regulation of the European Parliament and of the Council on credit rating agencies", COM(2008) 704 final. Brussels: European Commission.

European Commission 2009. "Approval of new Regulation will raise standards for the issuance of credit ratings used in the Community", Press Release IP/09/629. 23 April.

European Commission 2013a. "New rules on credit rating agencies (CRAs) enter into force: frequently asked questions", Press Release MEMO/13/571. 18 June.

European Commission 2013b. "Stricter rules for credit rating agencies to enter into force", Press Release IP/13/555. 18 June.

European Commission 2016. *Study on the State of the Credit Rating Market: Final Report*. Luxembourg: Publications Office of the European Union.

European Parliament, Council of the European Union 2006a. "Directive 2006/48/EC of the European Parliament and of the Council of 14 June 2006 relating to the taking up and pursuit of the business of credit institutions". *Official Journal of the European Union*, 30 June, L 177/1–200.

European Parliament, Council of the European Union 2006b. "Directive 2006/49/EC of the European Parliament and of the Council of 14 June 2006 on the capital adequacy of investment firms and credit institutions". *Official Journal of the European Union*, 30 June, L 177/201–55.

European Parliament, Council of the European Union 2009. "Regulation (EC) no 1060/2009 of the European Parliament and of the Council of 16 September 2009 on credit rating agencies". *Official Journal of the European Union*, 17 November, L 302/1–31.

European Parliament, Council of the European Union 2013a. "Directive 2013/14/EU of the European Parliament and of the Council of 21 May 2013 amending Directive 2003/41/EC on the activities and supervision of institutions for occupational retirement provision, Directive 2009/65/EC on the coordination of laws, regulations and administrative provisions relating to undertakings for collective investment in transferable securities (UCITS) and Directive 2011/61/EU on Alternative Investment Funds Managers in respect of over-reliance on credit ratings". *Official Journal of the European Union*, 31 May, L 145/1–3.

European Parliament, Council of the European Union 2013b. "Directive 2013/36/EU of the European Parliament and of the Council of 26 June 2013 on access to the activity of credit institutions and the prudential supervision of credit institutions and investment firms, amending Directive 2002/87/EC and repealing Directives 2006/48/EC and 2006/49/EC". *Official Journal of the European Union*, 27 June, L 176/338–436.

European Parliament, Council of the European Union 2013c. "Regulation (EU) no 462/2013 of the European Parliament and of the Council of 21 May 2013 amending Regulation (EC) no 1060/2009 on credit rating agencies". *Official Journal of the European Union*, 31 May, L 146/1–33.

Ferri, G., L.-G. Liu & J. Stiglitz 1999. "The procyclical role of rating agencies: evidence from the east Asian crisis". *Economic Notes* 28 (3): 335–55.

Fimalac 2004. "History of the Group". In *2004 Annual Report*, 12–13. Paris: Fimalac.

Fimalac 2014. "Fimalac va céder 30% de Fitch Group à Hearst." Press Release, 12 December 2014. http://hugin.info/143461/R/1879679/662793.pdf.

Fimalac 2016. *2016 Annual Report*. Paris: Fimalac.

Financial Times 2011. "Fitch close to junking Portugal". 1 April. Available at: www.ft.com/content/65e7c37b-43f2-3db8-a464-376a5fce28c9.

Financial Times 2018a. "Hearst pays $2.8bn to take full control of Fitch Group". 12 April. Available at: www.ft.com/content/6f11d246-3e52-11e8-b7e0-52972418fec4.

Financial Times 2018b. "Fitch and S&P to launch China credit-rating units". 25 May. Available at: www.ft.com/content/fe73cb46-5fc8-11e8-9334-2218e7146b04.

Financial Times 2019a. "Corporate defaults in China surge in 2019 to record high $18.6bn". 26 December. Available at: www.ft.com/content/068a83e0-27a7-11ea-9305-4234e74b0ef3.

Financial Times 2019b. "S&P route into China's $12tn bond market faces perils". 31 January. Available at: www.ft.com/content/b95471d8-23a8-11e9-b329-c7e6ceb5ffdf.

Fitch Ratings 2002. "Fitch sovereign ratings: rating methodology". New York: Fitch Ratings.

Fitch Ratings 2012. "Sovereign rating criteria: master criteria". 13 August.

Fitch Ratings 2013a. "Definitions of ratings and other forms of opinion". July.

Fitch Ratings 2013b. "Fitch downgrades Italy to 'BBB+'; outlook negative", press release. 8 March. Available at: www.fitchratings.com/research/sovereigns/fitch-downgrades-italy-to-bbb-outlook-negative-08-03-2013.

Fitch Ratings 2014. "UK: rating implications of Scottish independence", special report. London: Fitch Ratings.

Fitch Ratings 2018. "Sovereign rating criteria: effective from 19 July 2018 to 27 May 2019". 19 July. Available at: www.fitchratings.com/research/sovereigns/sovereign-rating-criteria-effective-from-19-july-2018-27-may-2019-19-07-2018.

Fitch Ratings 2020. "Rating definitions", special report. London: Fitch Ratings.

FSB 2010. "Principles for reducing reliance on CRA ratings". Basel: FSB.

FSB 2012a. "Roadmap and workshop for reducing reliance on CRA ratings". 5 November. Available at: www.fsb.org/wp-content/uploads/r_121105b.pdf.

FSB 2012b. "Overview of progress in the implementation of the G20 recommendations for strengthening financial stability". Basel: FSB.

FSB 2013. "Credit rating agencies: reducing reliance and strengthening oversight: progress report to the St Petersburg G20 summit". 29 August. Available at: www.fsb.org/wp-content/uploads/r_130829d.pdf.

FSB 2014. "Peer review report: thematic review on FSB principles for reducing reliance on CRA ratings". Basel: FSB.

Fuchs, A. & K. Gehring 2013. "The home bias in sovereign ratings", paper presented at the American Political Science Association annual meeting, 1 September [updated version: December].

Fuchs, A. & K. Gehring 2015. "The home bias in sovereign ratings", Discussion Paper 179. Göttingen: Courant Research Centre: Poverty, Equity and Growth in Developing and Transition Countries, Georg-August-Universität Göttingen.

Fuchs, A. & K. Gehring 2017. "The home bias in sovereign ratings". *Journal of the European Economic Association* 15 (6): 1386–423.

Gabor, D. & C. Ban 2014. "Fiscal policy in financialized times: investor loyalty and financialization in the European financial crisis", manuscript prepared for 21st International Conference of Europeanists, 14–16 March, Washington, DC.

Gabor, D. & C. Ban 2015. "Banking on bonds: the link between states and markets". *Journal of Common Market Studies* 54 (3): 617–35.

Gaillard, N. 2012. *A Century of Sovereign Ratings*. Berlin: Springer.

Gaillard, N. 2014. "How and why credit rating agencies missed the eurozone debt crisis". *Capital Markets Law Journal* 9 (2): 121–36.

Gaillard, N. & W. Harrington 2016. "Efficient, commonsense actions to foster accurate credit ratings". *Capital Markets Law Journal* 11 (1): 38–59.

Gärtner, M. & B. Griesbach 2012. "Rating agencies, self-fulfilling prophecy and multiple equilibria? An empirical model of the European sovereign debt crisis 2009–2011", Economics Working Paper 1215. St. Gallen: School of Economics and Political Science, University of St. Gallen.

Gärtner, M., B. Griesbach & F. Jung 2011. "PIGS or lambs? The European sovereign debt crisis and the role of rating agencies". *International Advances in Economic Research* 17 (3): 288–99.

GIC 2018. "GIC invests in Lianhe Ratings". 29 January. Available at: www.gic.com.sg/newsroom/news/gic-invests-in-lianhe-ratings.

Gras, I. 2005. "Rating-Agenturen und Kapitalmarktentwicklung in der VR China", China Analysis 46. Trier: University of Trier.

Guardian 2009. "The world according to Standard & Poor's". 22 May. Available at: http://image.guardian.co.uk/sys-files/Guardian/documents/2009/05/22/Creditrating.pdf.

Guardian 2011. "Ireland's credit rating downgraded again". 2 February. Available at: www.theguardian.com/business/2011/feb/02/ireland-credit-rating-downgraded.

Guardian 2012. "Eurozone crisis live: China tells Europe to 'do its homework'". 2 February. Available at: www.theguardian.com/business/2012/feb/02/eurozone-crisis-greecedebt-negotiaions.

Guzzini, S. 2010. "Power analysis: encyclopedia entries", Working Paper 2010:34. Copenhagen: Danish Institute for International Studies.

Hackhausen, J. 2012. "Das Märchen von der amerikanischen Verschwörung". *Handelsblatt*, 17 January.

Harold, G. 1938. *Bond Ratings as an Investment Guide: An Appraisal of Their Effectiveness*. New York: Ronald Press.

Harrington, B. 2020. "Investors who want to fast-track sustainable fixed income investments should inundate credit rating agencies with methodology critiques". Responsible Investor, 28 January. Available at: www.responsible-investor.com/articles/investors-who-want-to-fast-track-sustainable-fixed-income-investments-should-inundate-credit-rating-agencies-with-methodology-critiques.

Hearst 2019. "Hearst president & CEO reflects on the record year". 22 January. Available at: www.hearst.com/-/hearst-president-ceo-reflects-on-the-record-year.

Henning, C. & A. Walter (eds) 2016. *Global Financial Governance Confronts Emerging Powers*. Waterloo, ON: Centre for International Governance Innovation.

Hinrichs, T. 2012. "Dann wüssten wir auch die Lotto-Zahlen", interview by Lukas Kapeller. *Der Standard*, 16 January.

Hiss, S. & S. Nagel 2014. "Credit rating agencies". In *Europe and the Governance of Global Finance*, D. Mügge (ed.), 127–40. Oxford: Oxford University Press.

Hull, J., M. Predescu & A. White 2004. "The relationship between credit default swap spreads, bond yields, and credit rating announcements". *Journal of Banking & Finance* 28 (11): 2789–811.

IMF 2010. "The uses and abuses of sovereign credit ratings". In *Global Financial Stability Report: Sovereigns, Funding, and Systemic Liquidity*, 87–122. Washington, DC: IMF.

IOSCO 2003a. "IOSCO statement of principles regarding the activities of credit rating agencies". 25 September. Available at: www.iosco.org/library/pubdocs/pdf/IOSCOPD151.pdf.

IOSCO 2003b. "Report on the activities of credit rating agencies". Madrid: IOSCO.

IOSCO 2004. "Code of Conduct Fundamentals for Credit Rating Agencies". Madrid: IOSCO.

IOSCO 2015b. "IOSCO Issues Fnal Code of Conduct Fundamentals for Credit Rating Agencies", Media Release MR/14/2015. 24 March. Available at: www.iosco.org/news/pdf/IOSCONEWS375.pdf.

Katz, M. & C. Shapiro 1985. "Network externalities, competition, and compatibility". *American Economic Review* 75 (3): 424–40.

Kennedy, S. 2008. "China's emerging credit rating industry: the official foundations of private authority". *China Quarterly* 193: 65–83.

Kennedy, S. 2019. "In China's credit ratings, democracies pay a price". Foreign Policy, 8 August. Available at: https://foreignpolicy.com/2019/08/08/976045-china-dagong-credit-credit-ratings-democracy.

Kiff, J., S. Nowak & L. Schumacher 2012. "Are rating agencies powerful? An investigation into the impact and accuracy of sovereign ratings", Working Paper 12/23. Washington, DC: IMF.

Kirkland, E. 1961. *Industry Comes of Age: Business, Labor and Public Policy, 1860–1897*. New York: Holt, Rinehart & Winston.

Kovach, B. & T. Rosenstiel 1999. *Warp Speed: America in the Age of Mixed Media*. Washington, DC: Brookings Institution Press.

Krippner, G. 2011. *Capitalizing on Crisis: The Political Origins of the Rise of Finance*. Cambridge, MA: Harvard University Press.

Krugman, P. 2010. "Berating the raters". *New York Times*, 25 April.

Lall, R. 2012. "From failure to failure: the politics of international banking regulation". *Review of International Political Economy* 19 (4): 609–38.

Langohr, H. & P. Langohr 2008. *The Rating Agencies and Their Credit Ratings: What They Are, How They Work, and Why They Are Relevant*. Boston: Wiley.

Levey, D. & S. Brown 2005. "The overstretch myth: can the indispensable nation be a debtor nation?". *Foreign Affairs* 84 (2): 2–7.

McCloskey, D. 1983. "The rhetoric of economics". *Journal of Economic Literature* 21 (2): 481–517.

MacKenzie, D. 2006. *An Engine, Not a Camera: How Financial Models Shape Markets*. Cambridge, MA: MIT Press.

McVea, H. 2010. "Regulating credit rating agencies in the European Union: where might it lead?". *Amicus Curiae* 83 (autumn): 2–6.

Manaigo-Vekil, A. 2012. "The regulation of credit rating agencies in Europe and ESMA's supervisory power". *Columbia Journal of European Law* 18: 34–45.

Marandola, G. & T. Sinclair 2014. "Credit rating agencies: a constitutive and diachronic analysis", SPERI Paper 16. Sheffield: Sheffield Political Economy Research Institute, University of Sheffield.

Marandola, G. & T. Sinclair 2017. "Credit rating agencies are poorly understood and the rules developed for them will not work". In *Handbook on the Geographies of Money and Finance*, R. Martin & J. Pollard (eds), 478–96. Cheltenham: Edward Elgar.

Mathis, J., J. McAndrews & J.-C. Rochet 2009. "Rating the raters: are reputation concerns powerful enough to discipline rating agencies?". *Journal of Monetary Economics* 56 (5): 657–74.

Mattarocci, G. 2014. *The Independence of Credit Rating Agencies: How Business Models and Regulators Interact*. Amsterdam: Academic Press.

Mehrling, P. 2010. *The New Lombard Street: How the Fed Became the Dealer of Last Resort*. Princeton, NJ: Princeton University Press.

Mennillo, G. 2016. "Sovereign ratings and the solvency of states: a case of structural power". PhD dissertation, University of St. Gallen.

Mennillo, G. 2020. "He who pays the piper calls the tune: and the 'relocation of the world's credit rating center' goes to?". In *BRICS and the Global Economy*, S. Y. Kim (ed.), 229–58. Singapore: World Scientific.

Mennillo, G. & S. Roy 2014. "Ratings and regulation: a case of an irreversible marriage?", Working Paper 14-0004. Cambridge, MA: Weatherhead Center for International Affairs, Harvard University.

Mennillo, G. & T. Sinclair 2019. "A hard nut to crack: regulatory failure shows how rating really works". *Competition & Change* 23 (3): 266–86.

Mises, L. 1949. *Human Action*. New Haven, CT: Yale University Press.

Moody, J. 1933. *The Long Road Home: An Autobiography*. London: Macmillan.

Moody's Investors Service 2001. "Rating action: Moody's downgrades Enron Corp's long-term debt ratings (senior unsecured to B2); commercial paper confirmed at not-prime; ratings remain under review for downgrade". 28 November. Available at: www.moodys.com/research/MOODYS-DOWNGRADES-ENRON-CORPS-LONG-TERM-DEBT-RATINGS-SENIOR-UNSECURED--PR_50940.

Moody's Investors Service 2002. *Moody's Country Credit Statistical Handbook*. New York: Moody's Investors Service.

Moody's Investors Service 2010a. "Rating action: Moody's downgrades Ireland to Baa1 from Aa2; outlook negative". 17 December. Available at: www.moodys.com/research/Moodys-downgrades-Ireland-to-Baa1-from-Aa2-outlook-negative--PR_211361.

Moody's Investors Service 2011. "Response to European Commission public consultation on credit rating agencies". 7 January. Available at: www.moodys.com/researchdocumentcontentpage.aspx?docid=PBC_129969.

Moody's Investors Service 2012. "Proposed refinements to the sovereign bond rating methodology: request for comment". 17 December. Available at: www.moodys.com/Pages/HowMoodysRatesSovereigns.aspx.

Moody's Investors Service 2013a. "Moody's publishes sovereign rating methodology", press release. 12 September. Available at: www.moodys.com/research/Moodys-publishes-sovereign-rating-methodology--PR_282238.

Moody's Investors Service 2013b. "Rating symbols and definitions". New York: Moody's Investors Service.

Moody's Investors Service 2013c. "Rating action: Moody's affirms Italy's Baa2 government ratings and negative outlook". 26 April.

Moody's Investors Service 2014. "Announcement: Swiss voters' decision to curb immigration is credit negative for Switzerland and Swiss banks". 18 February. Available at: www.moodys.com/research/Moodys-Swiss-voters-decision-to-curb-immigration-is-credit-negative--PR_293038?WT.mc_id=NLTITLE_YYYYMMDD_PR_293038.

Moody's Investors Service 2017. *Annual Report 2017*. New York: Moody's Investors Service.

Moody's Investors Service 2018a. "Rating methodology, sovereign & supranational". 27 November.

Moody's Investors Service 2018b. "Rating methodology, regional and local governments, sub-sovereign". 16 January.

Moody's Investors Service 2019. "Rating action: Moody's changes Daimler's outlook to negative, A2 ratings affirmed". 31 July. Available at: www.moodys.com/research/Moodys-changes-Daimlers-outlook-to-negative-A2-ratings-affirmed--PR_405230.

Moody's Investors Service 2020a. "Rating symbols and definitions". New York: Moody's Investors Service.

Moody's Investors Service 2020b. "Rating action: Moody's places ratings of 7 European automotive manufacturers on review for downgrade one issuer for direction uncertain; downgrades one issuer". 25 March. Available at: www.moodys.com/research/Moodys-places-ratings-of-7-European-Automotive-manufacturers-on-review--PR_420407.

New York Times 1908. "Henry W. Poor fails; loss over a million". 27 December.

New York Times 2011. "Markets turn higher after Berlusconi offers to resign". 8 November.

New York Times 2013. "Fitch downgrades Italian debt, citing political turmoil". 8 March.

New York Times 2019. "China's companies binged on debt. Now they can't pay the bill". 12 December.

Nölke, A. & J. Perry 2007. "The power of transnational private governance: financialization and the IASB". *Business and Politics* 9 (3): 1–25.

Ouroussoff, A. 2010. *Wall Street at War: The Secret Struggle for the Global Economy*. Cambridge: Polity.

Partnoy, F. 2003. *Infectious Greed: How Deceit and Risk Corrupted the Financial Markets*. New York: Times Books.

Paudyn, B. 2013. "Credit rating agencies and the sovereign debt crisis: performing the politics of creditworthiness through risk and uncertainty". *Review of International Political Economy* 20 (4): 788–818.

Persaud, A. 2008. "The inappropriateness of financial regulation". VoxEu, 1 May. Available at: www.voxeu.org/article/inappropriateness-financial-regulation.

Persaud, A. 2009. "What to do about credit rating agencies?". In *The Warwick Commission on International Financial Reform: In Praise of Unlevel Playing Fields*, Warwick Commission (ed.), 15–16. Coventry: University of Warwick.

Poon, M. 2012. "Rating agencies". In *The Oxford Handbook of the Sociology of Finance*, K. Knorr Cetina & A. Preda (eds), 1–16. Oxford: Oxford University Press.

Porter, T. 2014. *Transnational Financial Regulation after the Global Financial Crisis*. Abingdon: Routledge.

Pozsar, Z. *et al.* 2010. "Shadow banking", Staff Report 458 [rev. February 2012]. New York: Federal Reserve Bank of New York.

Quaglia, L. 2013. "Financial services governance in the European Union after the global financial crisis: incremental changes or path-breaking reform?". In *Great Expectations, Slow*

Transformations: Incremental Change in Post-Crisis Regulation, M. Moschella & E. Tsingou (eds), 57–75. London: ECPR Press.

Reisen, H. & J. von Maltzan 1999. "Boom and bust and sovereign ratings". *International Finance* 2 (2): 273–93.

Reuters 2009. "Publisher Hearst ups stake in Fitch ratings". 24 July. Available at: www.reuters.com/article/fimalac-fitch-idUSLO37889320090724.

Reuters 2011a. "France shocked by S&P downgrade error". 11 November. Available at: http://uk.reuters.com/article/uk-france-ratings-sandp-erroridUKTRE7AA12820111111.

Reuters 2011b. "United States loses prized AAA credit rating from S&P". 6 August. Available at: www.reuters.com/article/2011/08/06/us-usa-debt-downgrade-idUSTRE7746VF20110806.

Reuters 2012. "Hearst buys another 10 percent of Fitch for $177 million". 9 February. Available at: www.reuters.com/article/us-hearst-fitch-idINTRE8181LW20120209.

Reuters 2013a. "Dagong downgrades US to A– from A". 17 October. Available at: www.reuters.com/article/idUSL3N0I71YW20131017.

Reuters 2013b. "Debt limit row, government shutdown unlikely to hit US rating: Moody's". 24 September. Available at: www.reuters.com/article/us-usa-debt-moodys-idUSBRE98N0KW20130924.

Reuters 2019. "Chinese rating agency Dagong resumes operations after suspension". 4 November. Available at: www.reuters.com/article/china-bonds-ratingsidUSL3N27K1Z9.

Rivlin, A. & J. Soroushian 2017. "Credit rating agency reform is incomplete". Brookings, 7 March. Available at: www.brookings.edu/research/credit-rating-agency-reform-is-incomplete.

Roos, J. 2019. *Why Not Default? The Political Economy of Sovereign Debt*. Princeton, NJ: Princeton University Press.

Roubini, N. 2015. "Rating agencies still matter – and that is inexcusable". *Financial Times*, 10 August.

Rügemer, W. 2012a. "Der Rating-Komplex: wie Kapital- und Staatsmacht den Markt manipulieren". *Blätter für deutsche und internationale Politik* 57 (4): 71–82.

Rügemer, W. 2012b. *Rating-Agenturen: Einblicke in die Kapitalmacht der Gegenwart*. Bielefeld: Transcript Verlag.

SEC 2003b. "Report on the role and function of credit rating agencies in the operation of the securities market". Washington, DC: SEC.

SEC 2022. "Office of Credit Ratings Staff Report on Nationally Recognized Statistical Rating Organizations". Washington, DC: SEC.

Scalet, S. & T. Kelly 2012. "The ethics of credit rating agencies: what happened and the way forward". *Journal of Business Ethics* 111 (4): 477–90.

Schwarcz, S. 2002. "Private ordering of public markets: the rating agency paradox". *University of Illinois Law Review* 1 (18): 1–29.

Sheng, J. 2019. "The debt ratings debate and China's emerging credit rating industry: regulatory issues and practices". *Athens Journal of Law* 5 (4): 375–404.

Sinclair, T. 1999. "Bond-rating agencies and coordination in the global political economy". In *Private Authority and International Affairs*, A. Cutler, V. Haufler & T. Porter (eds), 153–67. Albany, NY: SUNY Press.

Sinclair, T. 2001. "The infrastructure of global governance: quasi-regulatory mechanisms and the new global finance". *Global Governance* 7 (4): 441–51.

Sinclair, T. 2005. *The New Masters of Capital: American Bond Rating Agencies and the Politics of Creditworthiness*. Ithaca, NY: Cornell University Press.

Sinclair, T. 2010. "Round up the usual suspects: blame and the subprime crisis". *New Political Economy* 15 (1): 91–107.

Sinclair, T. 2013. "Global financial crises". In *Issues in 21st Century World Politics*, M. Beeson & N. Bisley (eds), 80–91. Basingstoke: Palgrave Macmillan.

South China Morning Post 2019. "China's government takes control of US bashing credit rating agency Dagong, which rated US debt lower than Chinese issues". 18 April.

Der Spiegel 2013. "SPD-Kanzlerkandidat im Interview: Merkel muss endlich die Wahrheit sagen". 2 April.

Standard & Poor's 2012a. "How we rate sovereigns". 13 March.

Standard & Poor's 2012b. "Standard & Poor's ratings definitions". 22 June.

Standard & Poor's 2013a. "Country risk assessment methodology and assumptions". New York: Standard & Poor's.

Standard & Poor's 2013b. "Corporate methodology". New York: Standard & Poor's.

Standard & Poor's 2014. "Standard & Poor's ratings definitions". New York: Standard & Poor's.

Standard & Poor's 2017a. *Annual Report*. New York: Standard & Poor's.

Standard & Poor's 2017b. "Sovereign rating methodology". 18 December.

Stellinga, B. 2019. "Why performativity limits credit rating reform". *Finance and Society* 5 (1): 20–41.

Straits Times 2020. "China regulator suspends Moody's Chinese joint venture over Yongcheng default". 30 December. Available at: www.straitstimes.com/business/economy/china-regulator-suspends-moodys-chinese-joint-venure-over-yongcheng-default.

Strange, S. 1986. *Casino Capitalism*. Oxford: Basil Blackwell.

Strange, S. 1998. *Mad Money: When Markets Outgrow Governments*. Ann Arbor, MI: University of Michigan Press.

Süddeutsche Zeitung 2011. "Moody blues". 16 November.

Süddeutsche Zeitung 2013. "In den USA sind wir nicht wollkommen". 14 November.

Sylla, R. 2002. "An historical primer on the business of credit rating". In *Ratings, Rating Agencies and the Global Financial System*, R. Levich *et al.* (eds), 19–40. Amsterdam: Kluwer.

Tageszeitung, Die 2011. "Ideologie ist kein Masstab". 25 July.

Tarullo, D. 2013. "Shadow banking and systemic risk regulation", speech at the Americans for Financial Reform and Economic Policy Institute conference, Washington, DC, 22 November. Available at: www.federalreserve.gov/newsevents/speech/files/tarullo20131122a.pdf.

Tichy, G. 2011. "Did rating agencies boost the financial crisis?". *Intereconomics* 46 (5): 232–45.

Wall Street Journal 2011. "EU wants ratings firms to relent on troubled nations". 21 October.

US Congress 2006. "Credit Rating Agency Reform Act of 2006". Public Law 109–291, 109th Congress, S. 3850, 29 September.

US Congress 2010. "Dodd–Frank Wall Street Reform and Consumer Protection Act". Public Law 111–203, 111th Congress, H.R. 4173, 21 July.

Verma, S. 2015. "Bank regulation: 'Basel IV' sparks banker fury". Euromoney, 5 March. Available at: www.euromoney.com/article/b12klgs5681h0r/bank-regulation-basel-iv-sparks-banker-fury.

Vernazza, D., E. Nielsen & V. Gkionakis 2014. "The damaging bias of sovereign ratings", Global Themes: Economics Research 21. London: UniCredit.

Weaver, D. *et al.* 2007. *The American Journalist in the 21st Century: US News People at the Dawn of a New Millennium*. New York: Routledge.

INDEX